JOSEPH FINK

LLOYD G. SEALY

The Community and the Police— Conflict or Cooperation?

A WILEY-INTERSCIENCE PUBLICATION

JOHN WILEY & SONS

New York · London · Sydney · Toronto

Library of Congress Cataloging in Publication Data:

Fink, Joseph, 1915-
   The community and the police—conflict or cooperation?

   "A Wiley-Interscience publication."
   Bibliography: p.
   1. Public relations—Police. 2. Police.
3. Team policing. I. Sealy, Lloyd G., joint author.
II. Title.

HV7936.P8F56   659.2'9'3632   74-1144
ISBN 0-471-25894-6

Printed in the United States of America

10 9 8 7 6 5 4 3 2 1

Foreword

I welcome this worthwhile contribution to the growing
literature on improving the effectiveness of our nation's
police departments. As a national legislator with committee responsibilities in the area of crime and delinquency prevention, I am well aware of the increased
demands that are being placed on the individual policeman in our society. Some would have us believe that every
problem of public safety in our cities could be solved
by just a few more policemen or better equipment in their

hands. Others focus all their attention on the abuses of power by police officers without examining the underlying causes of that problem. In such an atmosphere, it is encouraging to find a book such as *The Community and the Police—Conflict or Cooperation?* taking a thoughtful and fundamental approach to the problems of the police function.

Authors Fink and Sealy, two exceptionally qualified career police officers, are aware of the day-to-day problems of the police, especially the youthful rookie. They are aware of the experiments that have been attempted to improve the effectiveness of police officers. Their focus, however, is not on the police themselves but on the society which the police must serve. After examining in detail the personnel, the responsibilities, and the potential of modern-day law enforcement, they conclude that only by defining the role of the police officer in terms of the community he serves can real progress be made. The role they envision, moreover, involves a complete response by a qualified individual to all the problems of a community.

Now the overworked patrolmen and harried police administrators in this country are hardly going to welcome the news that the secret to success is merely to solve all the world's problems. They have been trying for too long to do the best they can on severely limited resources. If the basic premise of this book is accepted, however, the job of those law-enforcement officials will be made easier and not more difficult. That premise is that a policeman is more efficient when he is an integral part of a community than when he is an outsider.

The Community and the Police—Conflict or Cooperation? says what every good policeman has always known: to be an effective cop, you must understand and respect the people you deal with. Decisions are easier, actions are not counterproductive, and people cooperate when the man or woman on the beat is aware of the entire situation that is presented. Intense involvement with the community does not necessarily imply a complete departure from the traditional law-enforcement role. What it does imply is the ability to discern when a hard-nosed approach is out of line and a community service approach would better alleviate the situation. No matter how well intentioned or hard working a police officer is, if he or she does not have the awareness to make such a decision properly, a great deal of harm can be done.

This type of community awareness has become more difficult to obtain in modern times. It is almost a cliché to say that the pressures of our urban, technological world have created a society of individuals alienated from their neighbors. Such a consideration, however, is very relevant to the discussion in this book. It is difficult to ask a police officer to care about the community he works in when the members of that community themselves show mass indifference toward their common welfare. Too often the community-oriented policeman turns cynical when he begins to feel that he is the only one who cares. We cannot expect miracles of our police officers if we ourselves do not show some community involvement.

Neighborhood indifference is not the only problem. As Messieurs Fink and Sealy point out, there are structural problems within the police establishment itself which tend to erect barriers between the men and women in blue and the people they serve. For instance, too much emphasis on the military command model can tend to make a police department a closed circle. Policemen are, and should be, at war with crime. The dangerous situations they encounter require fast reactions. The problem arises when group morale becomes more important than public service.

Unfortunately, sometimes the pressures of constantly dealing with crime and criminals can lead policemen to
develop a distrust of all civilians.

Another roadblock to proper police–community relations
is the occasional excessive reliance on force by some
police officers. While society must protect itself against
its violent members, the use of force can quickly become
an improper crutch for a policeman who must face a wide
variety of complex situations. It only takes one or two
incidents of the misuse of violence to create an atmosphere of fear and suspicion where there should be trust
and cooperation.

These are not insurmountable problems, however. Good
police administrators can make their bureaucracies more
accessible to the public and can train their men and
women to keep the use of force to a minimum. The point
that the authors drive home is that any efforts to improve
police operations must have as their starting point a
proper definition of the policeman's community service
role. We cannot concentrate our efforts on the police departments because we will only be dealing with the symp-
toms of the problem. The real reason for police–community
hostility is that the police role has remained the same
while the needs of the community have been changing.
The police must be made an integral part of the community
if they are to be aware of the constantly changing needs
and expectations of their clientele.

The authors admit that defining the problem is easy. It is
the task of finding and implementing the solutions to problems that makes life difficult but interesting. The authors
take a very realistic, common-sense approach to con-
structing better police–community relations.

They examine in detail various police procedures that
have been successful in making the police an integral part

of the neighborhoods they patrol. The proposals they offer are simple: The basic idea is to make the police hierarchy more responsive to what is happening in the street. A decentralized power structure can make more intelligent personnel assignments and receive more community feedback. Giving well-trained patrolmen greater decision-making responsibility makes for better relations at the crucial point of contact between the police and the community. A patrolman can achieve an emotional identification with a neighborhood if he realizes that his daily decisions can significantly affect the welfare of individual people whom he has come to know well. The authors' examination of successful programs leads one to believe that good police–community relations need not be the exception. All that is really needed is a commitment to involvement on the part of police and community, and intelligent, persistent management efforts to achieve that goal.

A warning is necessary, however, lest the whole concept of a community police be tarnished by initial failures. It is not an easy task to remold an entire institution. As former high-ranking police officers, the authors of *The Community and the Police—Conflict or Cooperation?* are well aware of this. They realize that merely calling a policeman a "community conflict manager" instead of a "cop" does not change his role. Most experts seem to agree that police officers need more pay and training, but people must be willing to spend the money and set priorities for the type of training required. Community input at all levels of the police establishment is essential, but a disastrous experience with a hostile and incompetent civilian review board can make a police department even more distrustful of the general public. Blacks and members of other minority groups must enter the police ranks in increasing numbers, but we cannot expect them to be superhumans solving all a department's race-related problems. Women can vastly increase the efficiency of our police departments, but only if they are given access to all areas of police operations. All in all, the process of institutional change is a difficult task plagued with many potential setbacks.

The Community and the Police—Conflict or Cooperation? provides the groundwork for policemen, administrators, and the general public to begin working on a better relationship. Its basic tenets are difficult to dismiss, and they must be kept in mind if the police are to continue serving the cause of democracy rather than impeding it.

BIRCH BAYH
United States Senator from Indiana

Preface

In this book we take a critical look at the philosophy, concepts, principles, programs, and procedures that are being put into operation throughout the country to promote the view of the police officer as primarily a manager of community conflict.

Satisfactory human interaction in our complex, fragmenting, postindustrial society is increasingly difficult to achieve and seemingly almost impossible to maintain. Age-old and oft-tried remedies have seemed to be viable at times, yet have become ineffective at others. A science of problem solving that does not require constant observation, evaluation, and revision has yet to be devised. The manner in which we identify a socially desirable and effective police—and the role definitions that accrue from it—presents the same difficulties.

Preeminently, what is needed in a police occupation is a good deal of patience, understanding, and clear thinking. An empathic approach to the clientele is the *sine qua non* for developing a cooperative relationship. This is a valid enough judgment to make when we deal with logical and dispassionate people in situations free from aggression, tension, and the pressure-cooker qualities of life in urban environments. But what human scenes that require police intervention fit so benign a category? Few indeed.

Police are called to resolve disputes, arbitrate impasses, correct injustices, and calm contentious disputants. The incensed, the infuriated, and the belligerent are the habitual clientele of the police. Therefore, the art and craft of the public safety officer lies predominantly in conflict resolution. If such expertise is to come within the repertoire of every police officer, we need to develop and maintain a curriculum of techniques within the training apparatus, an armory of resources to support the patrolman while he is actually on the beat, and a problem-solving rather than tradition-maintaining orientation and philosophy on the part of the police administrators and middle managers.

Easier said than done. The task of the policeman, which has always been difficult, is today almost impossible. Nevertheless, it is clear that any attempt to provide police services to the community must be predicated on an understanding of the community's need for such services, the ability of the organization to provide such services, and the community's acceptance of the nature, quality, and intention of the services offered.

Given the social realities of the day, the tool that gives the most effective police service is not traditional law enforcement; it may be conflict management—the treatment of disruptive actions to resolve problems for the concerned individuals, groups, and subcommunities. To a large extent, successful conflict management depends on the capacity to relate to underlying causes or latent motivations that produce unusual, deviant, or antisocial behavior.

Conflict management as a vehicle for providing needed services can form the basis of an all-encompassing community relations system, operating throughout the entire police organization and strengthening the community by promoting programs in crime prevention, programs for exploring and influencing citizen attitudes toward law and justice, and action programs to correct environmental deficiencies in the community. The accompanying table lists the roles the policeman may assume as a conflict manager.

The growth of the central city, the megalopolis, and

THE POLICEMAN AS A CONFLICT MANAGER: Police Roles

Order Maintenance	Community Service	Law Enforcement
Keeping the peace	Health services	Warn and admonish
Regulation of conduct	Referrals to public and private agencies	Issue summons
Crime prevention	Civil law services	Make arrests
Settling disputes	Redress of grievances	
Crisis intervention	Emergency services	

interurban belts have multiplied the problems of government and administration. It has become increasingly difficult for police departments as presently constituted to hear the voice of the community crying out for aid, relief, or redress of inequities and infringement of basic civil rights. Sadly, law enforcement and the maintenance of public order—the most basic police services—are most desperately needed, yet most universally resented, in the slums and ghettos inhabited by the poor and by minority groups.

When the police can convince the people of their good intentions, which they can do only by earnest efforts and by responsible actions in the everyday performance of duty, they will merit and receive the confidence, respect, and cooperation of the citizens for the joint endeavor of shaping safer cities.

One thing is certain. Institutions must change with the needs and thinking of their clientele.

JOSEPH FINK
LLOYD G. SEALY

Pompano Beach, Florida
Brooklyn, New York
October 1973

Acknowledgments

It is rarely possible to prepare a study of this nature without the inspiration, encouragement, or assistance of many who consciously or not contribute to the *gestalt* of the work. Nor would this book have been possible without the experience of police careers for which we must acknowledge a debt to the City of New York and to the millions who tread its streets. Perforce, then, any listing of credits must omit many whose importance is unquestionable. We have had an opportunity to work in problem-laden communities that have provided insights and experiences we cherish and for which we are thankful. The enlightened administrations of New York's mayor, John V. Lindsay, Police Commissioner Howard Leary, and Chief Inspector Sanford D. Garelik, the ranking officer of the New York Police Department, made possible and likely our assignments to sensitive, challenging tasks.

Primarily, we are thankful and appreciative to Oscar Cohen, program director of the Anti-Defamation League of B'nai B'rith, for his confidence, guidance, and support. It is through his interest in police-community relations that this study was conceived, planned, and undertaken. Also because of his good offices we are able to acknowledge the assistance of Lilly Endowment, Inc., Indianapolis, Indiana, whose support made this work possible. We are also grateful to Robert Gordon, director of ADL's Indiana Regional Office for his cooperation and his assistance.

Academic inspiration and direction from the late Professor Claude E. Hawley and from Professors Leo Loughrey, Arthur Niederhoffer, Dr. Martin Symonds, and others in the administration and faculty of John Jay College of Criminal Justice of the City University of New York, aided us immeasurably. So did the education we received from the student body, whose reactions and comments led us on.

We are indebted, too, to our police colleagues: superiors, peers, and subordinates of the New York City Police Department, and to the many police officials and officers we encountered in our inspections, workshops, and conferences in other jurisdictions throughout the country. Especially helpful were Raymond Galvin of the Oakland, California, Police Department and John Angell of the Dayton, Ohio, Police Department. In Holyoke, Massachusetts, Mayor William Taupier, Deputy Chief Francis O'Connell, Captain George Burns, Jr., and Jack Goss were most cooperative.

Two without whom this book would have been impossible are Saul Braun and Stan Wexler, who gave their unstinted labor in research and editorial assistance. Our thanks also go to Dan Tumposky, who researched and recorded many of the initial inquiries into the subject matter.

Finally, to Sylvia Fink and Estelle Sealy, our wives, who also served by watching, waiting, and enduring, we record our thanks for their confidence, support, and Penelopean patience.

J. F.
L. G. S.

Credits

Permission to reprint the following material is gratefully acknowledged:

Quotation, p. 141: from Albert J. Reiss, Jr., "Police Brutality—Answers to Key Questions," *transaction*, New Brunswick, N.J., July/August 1968. Copyright 1968 Transaction Inc., p. 11.

Quotation, p. 41: from James Baldwin, *Fifth Avenue*

Contents

xxi

PART TWO   POLICE–COMMUNITY RELATIONS

PART THREE   COMMUNITY POLICE

The Community
and the Police—
Conflict or
Cooperation?

Part One
Police and Community

1. Who Is the Policeman?

It is hardly likely that police recruits will conform in all ways to any pattern. Nevertheless a profile can be drawn, based on our own years of experience on the New York City Police Department and on the results of numerous studies, that fairly reflects the social and psychological realities of police life.

The young man in question—he is about 24 or 25—is of average intelligence.[1] He has most likely worked at some sort of middle-class job before entering the police service, for perhaps a year or two.[2] However, a more meaningful indicator of his place on the socioeconomic scale is his background, which is likely to have been a low to medium income, lower-middle working class family imbued with the Protestant work ethic (the belief in the Calvinistic theory that hard work and dedication to duty are the surest means through which to achieve both success and salvation).[3]

Such a background will tend to encourage a certain ethnocentricity and a bias, having both economic and social foundations, against minority groups in general and blacks in particular. It will encourage a physical rather than a verbal method of resolving conflicts. A policeman raised in such a household would tend to communicate with his clientele in an authoritarian and paternalistic manner and would assume that citizens could not be expected to be compliant without "discipline" and "control." This police officer would be preoccupied with such matters as verifying his masculinity and maintaining his self-respect when challenged. Most researchers believe that these elements in an officer's background and early training can lead to a pronounced rigidity of personality, that is perhaps undesirable in the performance of police tasks.[4]

Why has this fellow chosen to join the police force?

Not, as some have supposed, because he has a violence-loving and authoritarian personality. Despite the manner he affects, the policeman is no more prone to violence and possibly is a less authoritarian person than others who were raised and educated as he was. Instead, he has chosen to be a cop primarily for security. Although he is strong and athletic, he is not what you would call an adventurous or devil-may-care fellow. On the contrary, he is a cautious and conservative man, both in his politics and in his moral nature. He has married early attempting, in a sense, to create for himself a stable, secure, and domestic environment.[5]

He himself does not feel any need to alter the status quo; rather, he sees himself as the defender of the status quo. Any political or moral challenge to authority seems to him at best antisocial and at worst treasonous. After all, *he* does not confront authority, he merely obeys it. For that, in essence, is a critical component of his identity. Basically a decent, obedient, law-abiding person, he is one who would like to live in a well-ordered society in which people respect the law and respect the law-enforcement officer as well. It does not take our rookie long to discover that inside the department, as well as in the larger society, there are many who do not share his attitudes. The oft-noted police traits of cynicism and suspiciousness are largely the result of this disillusioned idealism.

What exactly does the rookie cop experience that has such a deleterious effect on his personality? It is the painful process of discovering that the beliefs and virtues that he was taught to respect do not, in fact, reflect the reality of the world around him. For most people, this discovery takes place during adolescence. But Dr. Martin Symonds, Consultant Psychiatrist, Medical Unit of the New York City Police Department, and himself a former policeman, notes that cops are typically people who "seem to have side-stepped the adolescent process and have gone from childhood directly to adulthood." That is, they seem to have muted or suppressed altogether the period of rebelliousness and questioning of authority. "These young men are idealistic," Symonds goes on, "and have preserved an attitude towards authority that is one of respect, awe and sometimes reverence." [6]

Even as recently as his days in the police academy, our young policeman continued to be inculcated with values and beliefs of an unremittingly idealistic nature—such as the idea that he has taken on the majesty of the law and is responsible for law enforcement. Of course that is true. Should there be an altercation at a bar, suddenly our off-duty rookie is no longer off duty. If a man becomes drunk and obstreperous when the rookie policeman is at a party, all the other guests will turn to him to handle the incident. Suppose he is riding a subway car and somebody begins smoking; he personally may be no more annoyed by the cigarette smoke than anybody else in the car, but he is the one who is expected to deal with the situation. Should he find himself at a party where a joint is being passed, the discovery of his identity would produce more up-tight vibrations than would the presence of a doctor or a priest or a candidate for Congress. In folk wisdom and in estab-lished practice, and in the mental expectations of every-body, the policeman, on duty or off, is there to enforce the law. His presence takes on symbolic overtones that are assumed by members of few other professions. He *is* the law.

Much to his dismay, however, the rookie soon discovers that he is no more the law than anybody else is. This is not the case because of any personal failings—the same is true of everybody around him. And the same is true of the police institution itself.

In the United States in the 1970s, not long after he reaches his first assignment in a precinct, our rookie may find himself enforcing with respect to citizens a law that he *knows* his fellow officers are breaking and about which he is expected, by the most deeply engrained tradition of the institution itself, to say nothing.

The young police officer learns what it means to be a cop through a process that is a combination of experien-tial learning and informal socialization. The process has some positive aspects, but unfortunately the negative components far outweigh them.

The process of informal socialization consists mainly of repudiations of the formal training that the rookie has only recently received, immortalized in the time-honored police slogan, "You can't believe what they tell you at the academy. That's not the way it's *done*." This process encourages a profile of characteristics (secrecy, defensiveness, cynicism) which, once assumed by the young officer, alienates him totally from the larger society.

Unfortunately, nothing in the rookie's formal training program prepares him for this experience, which exacts a staggering toll on the young officer's self-image. Ask the typical cop and he may admit the truth: that being a police officer is a source of pride to him—or, at any rate, he once hoped and expected that it would be. He would have liked nothing so much as to live in a well-ordered society where people respected the law and respected him as its embodiment, thus making his job easier and more service-oriented, and winning him acclaim for the performance of his duties.

Alas, he is not acclaimed. He is criticized. He is disrespected. He is taunted and scorned. There is nothing a typical police officer dislikes so much as being criticized. It upsets him. It makes him extremely defensive. In some cases he is not as concerned as he should be to *be* blameless, but in all cases he is more than normally concerned to be *thought* blameless.

Every officer has had the experience many times of being confronted with the story of the cop who gave out a summons undeservedly, or asked for money, or was brutal or discourteous, or took graft. He is always, it seems to him, being put on the spot. And, naturally, he doesn't like having to carry around with him the fear that the finger will point to him. In other words, he needs to be more moral than anybody else; he bears the burden of being expected to show strength and courage and involvement far beyond anybody else, not only for himself but for the department. But what kind of training will strengthen him for that? In the current syllabus, none will.

From the inception of organized police forces, training of personnel has been a recognized necessity. But of what sort? Early American urban police agencies tended to utilize on-the-job experience as the sole training method. Several tours of duty alongside an experienced officer was considered sufficient introduction to the ways and means of law enforcement. Subsequently, through trial and error, the newcomer learned his duties, in however casual and idiosyncratic a manner, and he learned his limitations as well.

Classroom training of police recruits is relatively new. Only in the last 50 years has there been a trend toward formal training and police academies. Most large cities now have formal training programs for recruits; their type and extent depend on the size, resources, and philosophy of the particular agency—national, state, or local. The Police Training and Performance Study, a project report submitted to the Law Enforcement Assistance Administration in December 1969, shows a mean 697.9 hours of recruit training for the fifteen highest agencies out of a sample group of 60, and 217.9 hours for the fifteen lowest.[7] There is little variation in subject matter between the fifteen most instructive academies and the fifteen least instructive. Both groups stress Patrol and Traffic Training, Criminal Law, Evidence, and Investigations—that is, vocational aspects of police work. These constitute about 50 percent of the training. Firearms training and physical education consume another 20 percent of the training.

An additional 10 percent is spent on indoctrination into the policies and procedures of the department. The very small balance is devoted to client-oriented services, such as community relations (6 percent), first aid (4 percent), and the like.

Nevertheless, the latest recruit training syllabus of the New York City Police Department says it is geared to ensure that police officers will be "more functionally proficient, much more aware of the society in which they work, and their role in the community as both law enforcement officers and citizens." [8]

Is this true? Our rookie's formal training seeks to perpetuate all the high ideals and aspirations with which, presumably, he entered the force. It is, in other words, largely hortatory and doctrinaire. Thus in perhaps the most important sense the rookie is not prepared for the realities of police life in which the informal socializing process—intrinsically antithetical to all his prior training—becomes the single greatest influence on his character and career development.

In the informal training are concentrated the ancient but not always benign traditions of the service and the overwhelming peer group pressures that will affect to the strongest degree the previously held attitudes of the young officer. Many, if not most, become cynical. Most, if not all, soon discover that there is virtually no way for them to buck the system, no matter how distasteful they may find it, without grievously harming their careers.

When our rookie is assigned to a precinct, he is paired with an older, more experienced man. The assumption is that the senior man will teach the newcomer. In practice, very few of the older men take this educational role seriously. In many precincts, the most experienced officers will not even talk to the new men, since they don't want to introduce them prematurely to the benefits they hold as old-timers. Thus the new man receives the necessary indoctrination gradually over a long period of time, mainly from officers only slightly more experienced than he is.

Some of the information that comes to the rookie is vocationally meaningful, but much of it has to do with ways to outwit the sergeant, means of impressing citizens that the policeman is doing them personal favors, and other such police arcana. For example, the more seasoned man would certainly be sure to inform his younger colleague of the sad reality that gamblers are influential on the political scene. Or perhaps the youngster may find it out for himself, in a ruder fashion, after he makes the mistake of arresting important policy numbers people: soon afterward his assignment is altered and he is no longer in a position to arrest people it is impolitic for him to arrest.

As for the older officer with whom he is paired on patrol, his instinct (and frequently his practice) is to walk the rookie over to the neighborhood movie house and seat him in the last row, whispering, "Just sit there and don't get into no trouble. I'll call you when I need you." For many months, the older officer is less interested in teaching the younger man than in testing him. The rookie is on probation.

Is the younger man on probation until the older officer can see how good he is going to be at law enforcement? Yes, to a certain extent. But primarily the new cop is on probation until it can be seen whether he can keep his mouth shut. Is he an eager beaver? Is he a blabberer? Can he be depended on to be discreet? The hand of friendship, and a benevolent welcome onto the force, is not extended toward the rookie until it can be ascertained that he won't be going back to the sergeant, or to other officers, with information the older officer would prefer to keep a secret.

What would the senior man prefer to keep a secret? Well, our rookie, having passed the test, soon finds out. And of course he is highly motivated to pass the test, because above all else he is seeking to establish himself as part of the team. He is energetically on the lookout for clues to the kinds of behavior that will enable him to be liked and accepted by the older officers.

The clues, which are not long in coming, are not all negative. The rookie is learning how stringently to enforce the law against street peddlers, how to react in a family fight or during a barroom altercation, what the parking ticket policy is. . . .

At the same time, a darker strain begins to enter the relationship between the two officers. The older man brings the rookie a pack of cigarettes or a lunch that he says was given to him for nothing. If the rookie accepts— an indication that perhaps he is prepared to play the game —he might be sent to accept a gratuity himself. The radio car pulls up to a restaurant. The younger man is told, "Hey, listen, go see the fellow with the mustache who's working the counter and tell him that Al sent you for two sandwiches."

The rookie soon discovers that corruption is not uncommon at this low level. He is not only learning how to deal with drunks and juveniles, he is learning where to go for a free coffee. Possibly he is soon learning how to shake down a contractor.

Suppose our rookie says to himself, "Hey, what am I doing? Do I want to be a part of this? Shouldn't I blow the whistle on it?" His next move depends entirely on how strongly he feels about the situation and how much strength of character he can muster against overwhelming pressures. Because, above all, one policeman does not inform on another.

It must be emphasized that the police recruit is terribly vulnerable. He may have his own ideas about what constitutes proper behavior, but if it appears that the vast majority of the people in the organization he wishes to become a part of conduct themselves in some other way, he is apt to hesitate to say that they're all wrong. The pressure is especially strong since clearly analogous behavior is tolerated, condoned, and in some instances admired in the larger society. According to a recent survey in Boston, 70 percent of the sample believed that municipal corruption was prevalent, but only 2 percent thought that eliminating corruption was a possible area of improvement for city government.[9] Thus if corruption is a fact of life, our rookie tends to go along with it, if passively. Among new men observing graft, brutality, discourtesy, and violations of the rules of the department, most who feel uncomfortable tend to do and say absolutely nothing.

A few individuals are sufficiently strong minded and sure of themselves to speak up. If our rookie considered this possibility, he might say, "Look, I don't think that's the right thing to do. So don't do that if you're working with me. By yourself you can do anything you damn please, but I've got a share in the responsibility, so when you're with me I don't want that done."

In these rare cases, however, the protest is almost always directed to the partner, not to the supervisor. Even if he felt so inclined, the young cop realizes that he has almost no place to register a complaint and receive a fair hearing. He swiftly comes to feel that there's no point in trying to fight city hall. The findings of the Knapp Commission (a commission appointed in 1970 to investigate alleged corruption within the New York City Police Department) strongly suggested that it is much easier to go along with the system than to buck it, especially since the public itself tries hard to subvert the performance of young officers.

The rookie sits down for a meal at a restaurant counter. The owner comes over, pats him on the shoulder, and says that the meal is on the house. The new officer says, "No, thanks. I pay my own way." The restauranteur looks at him in amazement.

"Why should you refuse my generosity?" he asks. "The captain, the sergeant, all the men are my guests. You're all my friends. I'm not doing anything wrong."

Nobody is doing anything wrong, and yet the atmosphere is not one of openness and pride; instead, it is secretive and defensive. That is one reason for the unwillingness to be criticized and for the tradition that policemen do not inform on one another; that is why a "we" and "they" relationship is maintained with the public at large. That, too, is the primary source of the alienation of police from the larger society and of each level of the police hierarchy from those above it.

The young officer's acceptance of such practices—even though they contravene values he has held dear—is based on fear of such sanctions as ostracism and possibly even withdrawal of help while on duty. There is a point of great vulnerability for the rookie: Imagine how he feels when, in a brawl, he grabs a biceps that feels like a steel bar— and he is not sure that his partner will help him out. Failures to offer assistance are not unknown on the force if it is felt a cop is being disloyal to the code of the group.

If the recruit, let us say, told his older partner to go in and get his own free sandwich but to count him out, Al would surely go to the roll-call man and say, "Hey, you gave me somebody who isn't so hot. Don't put Charlie in the car with me any more." And he would tell his friends in the other patrol cars that the new man wasn't going along with the rules of the game. It has happened that the next time Charlie rapped three times with his nightstick to signal his need for help, Al shrugged his shoulders and said to himself, "Hell with him, he doesn't like the way I work, let him deal with the problem himself."

Some police agencies have attempted to counter this form of socialization by instituting the concept of the field training coach to reinforce the official ethos of the police department. A report on police, issued by the National Advisory Commission on Criminal Justice Standards and Goals, describes the training coach as "the most important element of an effective basic police field training program." [10] It recommends that a coach undergo training of at least 40 hours and emphasizes that the selection, training, and continued preparation of the coach are crucial because "the development of the new officer is in this man's hands." [11] The report also notes that "the best field officer will not necesarily become the best coach. While operational performance is one criterion, the ability to convey essentials of the job to others and the desire to develop new employees are at least as important." [12] Coordination between field training and classes is also singled out as important, particularly in large police agencies or in any agency experiencing rapid growth.

The current syllabus of the New York Police Department includes several hours on integrity, courage, responsibility, reputation, and other such matters, but only recently has police management been trying actively to promote these values. In the past, such concerns offered little more than lip service. Notable exceptions have been the efforts made by O. W. Wilson during his tenure as Chief of Police in Chicago, former Commissioner Patrick V. Murphy of New York, and Chief Edward Davis of Los Angeles, among others. There has been little real support for ideals that could only disturb the bedrock traditions of the force: that policemen support one another, that they don't rock the boat, that they refuse to testify against their fellow officers. Many men, so enveloped in the tradition that they cannot bring themselves to break it, thereby find themselves in the untenable position of arresting citizens for crimes their fellow officers are committing.

Consequently, our rookie's basically rigid and conservative personality has to (and does) undergo an interesting transformation that allows him to survive. He remains unyielding in his attitude toward citizen behavior, while becoming considerably more flexible insofar as police behavior is concerned.

The tenacity of the tradition of silence and the need to uphold the reputation of the department or agency was explicitly demonstrated during the Knapp Commission investigations into police corruption. Where reports of improprieties were submitted to high-ranking members of the department, there was a general reluctance to validate the charges, let alone investigate them. Many internal investigations within the police are unsuccessful because members of the department hesitate to inform on their peers. When an officer has been publicly exposed for wrongdoing, the universal sentiment is "There but for the grace of God go I." Even ranking officers assigned to internal investigations generally prefer to seek *sub rosa* terminations of behavior that might produce public scandal, rather than risk exposure.

One extremely serious effect of such practice is to destroy police credibility when citizen complaints are made against an officer. It is for this reason that the call is raised for civilian review boards. Internal procedures cannot possibly be taken seriously when the police habitually close ranks and when they fail conspicuously to be objective in dealing with complaints about police conduct.

In many communities, sadly, people do not bother to report complaints against police because they feel that no action will be taken and, beyond that, because they fear that the police will attempt harassment and retaliation against the complainants.

It is within this self-centered and self-enclosed bureaucracy that our young officer's career will either fade or flourish. Remember that his primary desire is for security and a place on the team. He is not one to challenge authority. His overriding goal is to perform well in the eyes of the rank immediately above him within the police hierarchy, and he is most likely to achieve this goal if, in addition to performing his duties well, he is compliant and responsive to the social environment.

In due course, then, the rookie discovers that all citizens need not be treated identically. If he has not already been so inclined, he may be socialized into treating some citizens with less courtesy than others. Whom can he treat discourteously with relative equanimity? The poor. The lower class. The drunk. The socially deviant. The sexually deviant. The blacks.

According to one theory, blacks are more likely to be mistreated by police because of innately racist attitudes. In another, it is because in most cities blacks lack political power. In a third hypothesis, the situation is thought to relate to class rather than race. Our guess is that all three are relevant. But there is another factor that is less frequently mentioned: namely, from the moment he receives his badge—and doubtless long before that—the typical policeman is operating under two assumptions.

One assumption is that a challenge to police is a challenge to authority, and a challenge to authority is itself a form of criminal behavior.

The second assumption is that the best way to deal with public disturbances—indeed, the *only* way—is with force. In some segments of the police establishment, it is still considered to be an object of faith that performance of police work is synonymous with the use of force. This is the more or less automatic assumption of the rookie, based partly on the prevalent conception of the police officer as the law enforcer and partly on his own subjective inclinations. By training, by orientation, and often by background, police are structured to be aggressive. When you ask them not to be aggressive in performing their duties, you are asking them to deny everything they have learned, everything they have come to trust. This can be summarized as: "It's our obligation to enforce the law and we'll use the force necessary to deal with any given situation."

To the extent that this view continues to predominate among police management in a society in which diverse voices are being raised even louder in protest, incidents of excessive or ill-applied force by police will continue to occur. The traditional way to deal with public disorder has been, shall we say, to wade in with the clubs. A police officer feels that he is capable of carrying out this tactic, and he is perfectly willing to do so. There may be some give and take, but he feels that in the end he will come out on top. He does not have to "stand there and take it."

Can nothing be done? Are "the police" always to be "the police"? Although traditionally police have been *primarily* law enforcers because that was (or was said to be) the most effective way of dealing with public disorder, must we now and in the future continue to view police *primarily* as law enforcers?

Various cities are conducting experiments to determine the effect on police behavior and self-image when an officer is not identified primarily as a law enforcer but as a professional whose chief responsibility is in the management of conflict. It remains extremely difficult to effect change of this kind, however, because most police interpret restraint as "muzzling." They see it as an attempt to diminish their ability to do the job.

To bring about this desirable change in attitude, it is essential, first of all, to show the officer that restraint can be more successful than force in performing his mission. Otherwise, the act of exercising restraint may be a positively humiliating experience. The policeman reasons as follows: "I, the representative of the law, have to stand here and be called everything under the sun and do absolutely nothing?" He says to himself, stewing, "What kind of man am I that I did nothing in this situation?"

The authors were able to identify these psychological factors firsthand, in 1968, in Brooklyn, New York, following the assassination of Martin Luther King, Jr. Large crowds had formed, some windows were broken, threats were hurled at the police, and at the corner of Nostrand and Fulton, more than 300 people, mostly young men, had gathered to vent their feelings about the murder and about white society in general. The police who were present naturally drew the ire of the demonstrators. Our options were to try to disperse the crowds or to engage them in direct confrontation.

In most street situations, the feeling of the men, and the traditional police approach, has favored the strong use of force, or a strong show of force, possibly followed by the use of force. In this instance, the police only remained on the scene, without responding to provocation with any type of aggressive response. This successful attempt to handle a potentially explosive situation and eventually to restore peace and tranquillity to the community with neither a large number of men nor the use of force became a learning experience for the men.

This is not to say, however, that there was not general mistrust of the policy of restraint. As the senior officer in the Brooklyn situation, I (L. S.) determined that we were going to try to avoid a physical confrontation, if possible; and I decided that it would be possible, provided no attempt was made to assault a policeman.

We had a sizable police presence on the corner of Nostrand and Fulton. The bulk of the men, however, were out of the immediate area, either in the armory on Atlantic Avenue or in patrol wagons nearby. As the crowd surged up and down the streets, the police walked a distance behind them, and patrol cars patrolled alongside the demonstrators to discourage looting. Other than that, however, the men took no action despite vilification and other provocations.

The tactical decision had been made by the highest-ranking officer present, and no discussion had followed. That did not prevent me from learning, however, that the men in the ranks believed that we were "coddling these people" and "letting them run away with this town." Such views typically reach the ranking officer through the hierarchy in the following manner.

The man in the ranks loses his temper and growls, "Hey, sarge, how long do we have to stand for this bullshit? What the hell are we coddling these people for?"

The sergeant, in turn, goes to the lieutenant and says, "Hey, lieutenant, some of the guys are wondering how far we go with this crap?"

The lieutenant mulls this over and approaches the captain. "Hey, boss," he says, "what happens when a cop gets hit by a bottle? Are we going to stand there and let them get away with it?" The captain, for his part, has been wondering just that. He goes to the inspector and tells him there has been grumbling from the men: "Is there any word from the top about when we can move or under what conditions we can move?"

The inspector goes to the ranking man at the scene and says, "Everything is going great now, but what do we do *if* . . . ?"

In that encapsulated form, a sensitive administrator can read a world of anxiety about police identity, police role, and police safety. In 1967, as it happened, the crowd began to thin out after a couple of hours of letting off steam. As the intensity of the community's passions diminished, the police were able to quell the disturbance without incident, and with a minimum of damage to property and injury to the people and the police. Restraint had paid off in police terms, but we lacked an instrument for analyzing and interpreting for the men the way in which police restraint had contributed to the success of the police mission. No such mechanism existed at the time because the primary view of the police officer not as a law enforcer but as a conflict manager had not yet been formulated. Consequently, there was no context into which to put the actual police street experience.

2. Who Is the Community?

Police–community problems are difficult for the police mainly because "community" is not as easy to identify as it first appears.

In the wake of the disturbances described in the previous chapter—and, indeed, all the social ferment of the late 1960s—spokesmen representing a considerable body of opinion could be heard complaining that the police had stood by "doing nothing" while damage to private property occurred and lawless behavior was observed. The same voices expressed themselves on behalf of an ever-increasing police presence and an ever-intensifying use of police force. They asserted with the greatest sincerity that the courts were "coddling criminals" and that purely because of political pressures police administrators could often be found in that reprehensible act of "pacifying the militants." Such views are often associated with those who identify themselves as supporters of police and who are thought to be friends of police in their difficult task of keeping order in the United States. But are they friends? Rhetoric should not be confused with action. James Vorenberg, executive director of the President's Commission on Law Enforcement and Administration of Justice, noted in 1972 three and one-half years after a strongly "pro-police" Administration entered the White House, "serious crime as measured by the FBI reports has increased by more than 30 percent to an all-time high in the nation's history. And in the case of violent crimes the increase is particularly disturbing. For example, reported murder and rape have continued to increase rapidly—rape by an alarming 25 percent in the nation's suburbs in a one-year period between 1971 and 1972." [1]

There is, then, a "community" of voices urging on police more of the same old tactics, the same old structures, the same tired approaches, which have not noticeably helped the police to solve their problems, and this community is considered to be friendly.

There is also a group of communities considerably more difficult to identify with precision except that they are unanimously critical of current police practices and philosophies and they are all considered to be unfriendly; in almost any given instance, they would like the police to do exactly the opposite of what the support-the-police community wants them to do.

Who, then, is this "community" everybody is talking so much about?

Is community the most vocal element in the police area of responsibility?

Is community the political and economic power base in the police area of responsibility?

Or is community the dominant ethnic or racial strain in the police area of responsibility?

Let us set aside for the moment the obvious fact that police are not neutral in the matter of what police practices and policies should be. Let us consider the problem of identifying "community" entirely apart from the police point of view. The problem remains, it lodges in the law itself, to the extent that it attempts to regulate political, economic, or social behavior. Community, no matter how we define it, will react positively to police activity that protects its interests and negatively when police activity is either a nuisance or a real intrusion on personal freedom.

For example, an unlicensed peddler sets up his wares on the sidewalk. He sees himself as a free-market individualist who is only trying to make a living. He has limited resources, perhaps, but he is an enterprising chap, and he can see no good reason why he should not be permitted to make his pitch. Now, along comes the cop on the beat. There is a law against unlicensed peddling, and depending on a number of factors, including precinct policy, the police response to the peddler can range from doing nothing at all, to inhibiting his efforts, to harassment, citation, and even arrest. If an arrest is made, the cop may believe that he has simply done his duty as a law-enforcement officer. He was just following the orders of his lawful superiors and seeing to it that illegal peddlers do not operate. But in fact the law may have been stringently enforced primarily because of intense pressure from local merchants. In that case, the cop was not merely enforcing the law, he was maintaining the peace of the community on behalf of one set of interests against another. There may or may not be legitimate "community" interests served by that particular law; but in either case, the police officer appears to the established merchant to be a sturdy, responsible fellow, doing his duty. To the peddler, the cop appears as the enemy of his freedom, the disturber of his peace, the abrogator of his natural rights.

This small example can be taken to represent all the extensive and complex social changes that have occurred during the past decade. If the peddler can somehow acquire enough political power to permit his voice to be heard in the councils where laws are made, he will swiftly become included within the definition of community. As soon as the peddler realizes that, you can expect to be hearing from him.

Thus the answer to the question "Who is the policeman?" is an evolving one, and so is the answer to the question "Who is the community?" During the past decade a number of publics have almost simultaneously awakened to their interests and have been organizing and verbalizing to assert claims to needs they feel are not being addressed by the larger society. Among these publics are blacks and other minority groups, women, youth, students, poor people, prison inmates, homosexuals, sexual deviants, smokers of marijuana, readers of pornography, and so on.

Most policemen resent having to respond to all that input. Prior to the erupting 1960s, it must be recalled, it was extremely easy for the policeman to identify the community he served. It consisted of the mayor, the city officials, the political office holders, the society of merchants and property owners, and a certain number of well-dressed and well-behaved white people who were easy to spot. Everybody else was potentially a law breaker and therefore was subject to instant police mistrust and suspicion and, significantly more frequently, police abuse.[2]

That mental set is now beginning, slowly, to change. There was a time, for example, when the gambler was considered to be an outlaw. Although statutory provisions relating to gambling remain on the books, community mores and in some cases official sanction have virtually legitimized such behavior. The neighborhood bookie or numbers collector is seen as providing a desired local service. One result is the newly legalized off-track betting facility in New York City. Another is the increasing reluctance of police administrators to expend the money and energy resources required to enforce all gambling laws. Former New York City Police Commissioner Murphy went on record as favoring the repeal of those laws relating to book-making and racehorse policy, proving once again that when community consensus is no longer attainable in a given area, the related laws become, for the police, virtually unenforceable.

The extreme reaction within the community to enforcement of laws that are at variance with community sentiment was manifested in Detroit in 1967, when serious rioting erupted following police action against an after-hours club in which liquor was being illegally sold. Extremely indignant, the community viewed the police action not as "law enforcement" but as harassment and the attempt to criminalize people who intended no antisocial behavior. The tragic end to which this impulse can lead was shown in the more recent events in the same city, when police broke into a social club. There was gunfire, and several persons were killed by the raiding officers. Subsequently it was learned that the patrons of the establishment were themselves police officers.

In these cases, the conflict is between laws that no longer (or never did) represent the community's best interests, and the community itself.

What of those instances in which the community splits into conflicting subcommunities? Both authors have attended local meetings of "community leaders," convened to give police administrators the benefit of their thinking, only to discover that one body of opinion objected to current levels of police presence, while another faction demanded an increase in police presence to deal with the hard-core crime in the neighborhood.

The problem of satisfying conflicting subcommunities intensifies when those involved cannot agree on what constitutes criminal or antisocial behavior. For example, on Memorial Day in 1967, on New York's Lower East Side, serious community conflict developed in Tompkins Square Park.

The neighborhood had long been a quiet, residential area. Succeeding waves of immigrants from Ireland, Italy, Eastern Europe, and Puerto Rico had come to the area, which had accommodated them more or less peacefully as they commenced their respective assimilations into American life. In the mid-1960s, however, the hippies arrived and apparently desired no cultural assimilation. They were young, uninhibited, and in many ways less rigid than the older neighborhood residents. Challenging traditional values and customs constituted a large part of their identity. Thus on Memorial Day the noisy frolicking, the casual nudity and sexuality, the dancing and singing of the hippies offended the older residents of the area, and the police were called to enforce park regulations.

In the ensuing fracas—which resulted from the hippies' belief that they were being treated unfairly and arbitrarily —scores were arrested and several people, police and civilians alike, were injured. Community tensions in an already polarized community were exacerbated. In this instance, no attempt was made to include the hippies in the definition of community and the result was, inevitably, increased community tension.

The incident served to notify the police that the young people in question had to be considered part of the community. It had become apparent that the police could not maintain public order successfully if they did not deal with the full community of those who were, for whatever reason, dissatisfied with police service.

As a result of many such incidents during the past decade, thoughtful, pragmatic police administrators recognized that the definition of community was being expanded, whether they liked it or not, to include those who had a right to expect parity of service but were not getting it. This included anybody who, in his dealings with police, had ever experienced discourtesy and verbal abuse, unresponsiveness, distance and impersonality of the institution, brutality and unnecessary use of force, abuse of authority and harassment, secretiveness and defensiveness, intolerance of dissent or deviance or cultural diversity, bigotry and bias, venality, and other characteristics that fall into one of two major categories: corruption or resistance to social change.

To the extent that an individual police officer incarnated any of the qualities just named, he could be said to have been contributing to the conflicts between the police and the community. Regardless of individual responsibility, however, it appeared to many within the newly awakened community that these corruptions were built into the system and could not be overcome, and that even if individual officers were decent, the police institution was inherently unresponsive. It became the responsibility of police administrators to prove that the critics were wrong.

For the police, the period of social disorder has been both a time of trial and a time for growth. During the past decade, police have (often grudgingly) begun to learn how far some of their basic assumptions could be stretched—chief among them, the premise that the need to maintain order in a community necessarily meant the use of force. Moreover, police have begun to discover that input from the community (even at the lowest, least powerful level) can be ignored only at the risk of encouraging public disorder. Police have learned that disorder, when it occurred, could not successfully be converted to order simply by the exercise of physical force in the name of an authority that failed to command the unquestioning respect it once had merited. If that authority no longer commanded respect, the police no longer could enforce law through evoking fear of authority in the community. That much was clear.

What was less clear was the answer to the question: If authority became less and less fearful and awesome to the ordinary citizen, what could be substituted to maintain the basic tenets of a civilized and law-abiding society?

How, in other words, could we survive as a society and not fall into total chaos and disorder if we could not *command* law and order? This book, in part, is an attempt to describe the development in the 1960s of the obvious alternative—a community-serving, democratic police. This problem-solving, conflict-managing police is not the idea of one man. It developed because a number of police officials and criminal justice theoreticians concluded that whereas the police could no longer successfully demand order, they could perhaps avoid having to shoulder all the responsibility for the task of achieving it by calling on the community to share in the work.

To the traditional police mind, this may sound like a capitulation of sorts. It may sound like a diminution of power. But, in fact, whenever the new orientation has been experimentally put into practice, the result has been increased, not diminished, authority to perform the police mission.

Part Two
Police-Community
Relations

---

3. Community Relations

In 1965, when I (L.S.) was commander of the 28th Precinct in Manhattan, an event occurred that led me to ponder the nature of the police relationship to the community—the direction from which it has come, and the direction in which, it now begins to appear, it must go.

One Friday early in the summer I was informed that a large, hostile crowd had begun to form in front of the Hotel Theresa at 125th Street and Seventh Avenue. The people were in a state of anger and frustration because payroll checks to be issued in connection with an anti-poverty (OEO) program of tree-planting for community beautification had not been properly countersigned and would not be issued until the following Monday. There had been a delay in processing. There had been some sort of administrative foul-up. The official empowered to countersign and release the checks had not gotten around to it in time.

Soon after I arrived at the scene, it was apparent to me that an incident of public disorder was due to explode. All efforts to persuade the people to clear the streets were unavailing, and the police presence in support of "public order" on behalf of a public agency that had through inadvertence, stupidity, or malfeasance, created a condition approaching public disorder, only managed to incense the people further. It became all too easy for them to redirect their animosity toward the police, who did not, in this instance, deserve it.

The notion of police as social lightning rod was more prevalent in past years than it is today; nevertheless, the police frequently find themselves inserted as a barrier between the agency attacked and the people attacking. It is their obligation to prevent destruction of property or injury to persons and to prevent the occurrence of unlawful acts, regardless of whether the behavior is a consequence of a legitimate social protest—and this circumstance alone exacerbates relations between police and community.

It is not unfair to say that in many instances both individuals and institutions have used and exploited the police as an instrument of repression. And it seldom occurs to the typical police officer to question whether this is the proper role for the police to play.

Additionally, there have not been, and there still are

not, any structures to enable the police to avoid this unde-sirable role if they choose not to play it. The commander of a police precinct has no jurisdiction over social service agencies in New York City, to keep them functioning prop-erly, but he does have a clear responsibility to maintain something like a condition of public tranquillity.

In the situation just cited, it would shortly have become incumbent on me to make arrests. And I certainly would have done so, all other options having become exhausted, despite my personal sympathies for the people who had gathered to vent their anger and frustration at being told they would have to spend the weekend without the money that was due them.

Yet these particulars were none of my business, as construed by me, by the police administrators above me who made police policy for the city of New York, and by the men below me who would, if necessary, follow my commands to disperse the crowds.

Fortunately, in this circumstance there was an alterna-tive path available to me, and I pursued it. Although it was a somewhat unorthodox procedure, I was emboldened by taking the overview that it was ridiculous for the police and the community to be at loggerheads because of an administrative snafu downtown.

I entered the building and informed the people in the agency that a riot was developing, that it could be stemmed only by the appearance of the delinquent official with a satchel filled with countersigned checks, and that as far as I was concerned, the individual involved had better make that appearance forthwith. Several urgent phone calls later he arrived, the checks were distributed, and the crisis was averted.

Pragmatically, the results were not at all to be feared or scorned. Order had been restored in a manner consistent with community needs. The policemen on the scene experienced a minimum of inconvenience and danger. And yet there are many police administrators who would have cleared the streets and made arrests, creating public order through an authoritarian exercise of police power—not because it would have been a superior solution to the police problem (clearly, it would not have been) but simply because they did not want to exceed their jurisdiction. In other words, they would have taken recourse to arrest as a strategy, knowing full well that it might have led to *increased* public disorder and *intensified* anger toward the police. Their reasoning would have been: our action represents *the furthest defined limit of the police role in the community*.

The anecdote just related exemplifies an insightful response to an emergency situation. In another instance, an enlightened police department took advance action to forestall negative popular reactions.

In December 1968 antiwar groups announced and planned for a series of mass demonstrations at the Whitehall Street Selective Service Induction Center in New York City. In preparation for this event, command personnel met with the demonstration organizers to establish lines of communication, set ground rules, and seek consensus on the scope of activities that could be construed as lawful protest and those which might be in violation of law. I (J.F.) was assigned to act as liaison between the demonstrators and the police commanders. My role was to ensure that the demonstrators were not deprived of their rights guaranteed under the First Amendment and that they would have immediate reception of complaints as well, thus avoiding events that might lead to disruptive situations.

Because of the special attention they received, the

demonstration leaders were more cooperative than many would have predicted. The press, too, found the attention given to this matter an interesting tactic on the part of the Police Department. This pro-active, or preventive aspect of our work also lies within the parameters of the police role. It typifies another dimension of successful conflict management.

In this book we attempt to redefine the limits of police role. We want to identify experimental models now operating that suggest desirable extensions of police identity into new areas, as well as certain once-traditional areas. At the same time that police have become highly bureaucratized and more efficient technologically, they have allowed formerly available options of tactics and strategy to be taken away. This has resulted in a lamentable rigidity in police operations that has made the police, in a more important sense, less efficient.

Arrest is one strategy for handling problems of public disorder. If arrest is the only strategy available, by all means use it. But if other options exist that can be used as effectively, or more effectively, arrest makes no sense. Yet, despite these options, arrest is as far as some police administrators can see. Not, as you might suppose, because of a lack of initiative (though perhaps a few police administrators are deficient in that quality) but primarily because the organizational structure within which they operate does not allow or encourage them to take functional responsibility at a local level. Thus they are often forced into a high-danger and low-yield strategy that is not very relevant to the reality of police life today.

In a similar context, field studies in Oakland, California, conducted within Chief Charles Gain's department, produced comparable conclusions, reported Assistant to the Chief Raymond Galvin:

In Oakland, we've done work in violence prevention
in the last three or four years. We talk about family
crisis, let us say, or landlord–tenant conflicts, or
community conflicts of any sort. We started out with
the idea that there are alternatives, but we tried not
to have preconceived values assigned to them. We
said to the officers, here's what's going on in the
situation and you're supposed to pick the best alternative for police response. The chief finally came to
the opinion that in the situations he was dealing
with, in the city of Oakland, under no circumstances
was arrest the best alternative. He made arrest the
last alternative.[1]

The Oakland policy notwithstanding, arrest, or the
threat of arrest, has always been assumed to be the
source of the policeman's authority, and it has indeed
been that. Seldom, until recently, has the question been
raised whether arrest was the best possible source of
police power. Historically, the police officer has been an
enforcer of laws who operates within a punitive crime-
prevention system, and it is a rare police administrator
even today who greets the search for alternatives with
great enthusiasm. Indeed, other sources of power probably were not at his disposal until very recently, and consequently an authoritarian presence and mode of behavior
was best. Within the last decade, however, it has become
transparently clear that if this was once the case, it no
longer is. The time has come for police to begin to break
loose from the assumptions that police ought basically to
be doing the work of law enforcement and that everything
else is "not real police work." The time has come for
police, acting purely from self-interest and with a view
toward the ultimate police objective—maintaining public
tranquillity—to set themselves broader goals. We should
not expect police to act other than in self-interest, be-

cause that is how everybody acts, in everyday situations. And police must not shrink from asking themselves whether the evidence before them has not already amply proved the need for basic structural and conceptual reorganization.

Such rethinking of roles and duties is by no means alien to today's police. Galvin remarked:

> I have very strong reservations about police organizations around the country. Some of them I'd be happy if we could just get them to be rational. For a lot of them, there's no real way to handle problems at all. The model we have usually used has placed emphasis on the detection and apprehension syndrome. They're investigative oriented. That's what the public is oriented to. People tend to believe that if you just arrest enough people that'll solve the problems, and policemen view detectives as a promotion up the ladder, and because of the emphasis on detecting criminals and arresting criminals the standard pattern of organization is just that. The detective division receives resources probably well beyond what it would merit if you were going to do a cost-analysis of detectives, because on a cost basis they are not a very efficient way of organizing. They just are not. People say the major problem of this city is crime control. That's not true in most cities. In most cities the major problem is something else. It's service. Oakland is very well organized and the policemen are quite convinced that they have reached nirvana as far as organization is concerned, but it's untrue, and the chief knows it's untrue. The men sit down and bitch about the things that are going wrong and so they know it's not perfection, but if you look at O. W. Wilson or the International City Managers' Association, it is. We do all the right things. The International Association of Chiefs of Police has five ex-Oakland police officers on the staff that go around telling people to organize

> this way. The problem is, it's not meeting what
> we've got to deal with on the street, and the only
> people that seem to be recognizing it are the people
> on the street, and the chief. Very few people in
> between.[2]

Galvin identifies here the understructure of what is finally being recognized as one of the two or three most urgent urban problems; that is, the dilemma of police and community.

In this context it is generally assumed that "community" is a euphemism for "race," but this is not accurate. Police have had community relations problems with people of a variety of ethnic and racial strains, and the common denominator appears to have been the distance between the people in question—whether Irish, Italian, female, laboring class, or sexually deviant—and political power. In May 1937 in South Chicago, to give one example, police acting in defense of the property of Republic Steel, killed ten people.[3] Those slain were CIO laborers participating in a sit-down strike in which they had taken possession of the premises, refusing to depart until their demands were met. Today, people of the counterculture, Puerto Ricans and, particularly, black people, are among the most visible indicators of this tension between those who desire a change of condition and those who, having changed their condition for the better, are concerned that there won't be room enough on the raft or, indeed, that there won't be any raft. In this dialogue, the police have been, and continue to be, expected to play an unattractive and socially undesirable role, though by and large most police do not yet see it that way.

The National Advisory Commission on Civil Disorders concluded in 1967 that riots in the cities invariably were precipitated by contacts between citizens and police[4] and that, in effect, many segments of our society share the perceptions recorded by black author James Baldwin:

> The only way to police a ghetto is to be oppressive. None of the police commissioner's men, even with the best will in the world, have any way of understanding the lives led by the people; they swagger about in twos and threes patrolling. Their very presence is an insult, and it would be, even if they spent their entire day feeding gum drops to children. They represent the force of the white world, and that world's criminal profit and ease, to keep the black man corralled up here, in his place. The badge, the gun in the holster, and the swinging club, make vivid what will happen should his rebellion become overt. . . .
>
> It is hard, on the other hand, to blame the policeman, blank, good natured, thoughtless, and unsuperably innocent, for being such a perfect representative of the people he serves. He, too, believes in good intentions and is astounded and offended when they are not taken for the deed. He has, never, himself, done anything for which to be hated—which of us has? And yet he is facing, daily and nightly, the people who would gladly see him dead, and he knows it. There are few things under heaven more unnerving than the silent accumulating contempt and hatred of a people. He moves through Harlem, therefore, like an occupying soldier in a bitterly hostile country. . . ."[5]

If police do not solve the dilemma of community relations, they cannot survive as an institution. And they cannot solve the dilemma without first decisively breaking with the view that their primary task is law enforcement. In some circumstances, in some communities, at certain times, it may be. In other circumstances, in other communities, and most of the time, it assuredly is not.

The rigid and inflexible view of police as enforcer of

law is a fairly recent innovation and does not represent the most traditional or even the most honored concept of police.

The earliest efforts at policing consisted mainly of the performance of watchman duties. The men worked only during hours of darkness, and their functions were only distantly related to law enforcement. They were obliged to be alert for fires, brigands, strangers in town, cattle breaking loose from their corral, and lost people abroad in the area under circumstances that might bring harm to themselves or to the community.

In New York City during the late nineteenth and early twentieth centuries, homeless individuals not uncommonly came to the police station for lodging. On cold nights they were let into the basement to sleep near the boiler, and in the morning they were offered coffee. Until perhaps 30 years ago, in addition to lodging, a small discretionary fund was maintained by each lieutenant in the station house, for distribution to the destitute or the dislocated. It can be seen from this cursory accounting that social service aspects of police work have more than a passing claim to attention.

The American police are an outgrowth of the British system, which was distinguished at its inception by the idea that local citizens' organizations, pledged to keep the peace, could handle the task of maintaining law and order. The concept clearly depended on the willingness of the citizen to be responsible not only for his own social behavior but for that of his neighbor, and to raise a hue and cry against the breaking of laws or local customs. Because the communities in question were small, homogeneous, and devoted to a traditional body of custom and culture, there was general unanimity on what constituted the breaking of a law or the flouting of conventional behavior. Thus the communities' involvement in the definition of unlawful or undesirable behavior guaranteed compliance with the police. This tends to be the case today as well, although coincidence of police and community definitions has somewhat diminished.

In Great Britain it is assumed that a bobbie will be courteous. In Syracuse, New York, by way of contrast, the arrival of a reform chief and his attempts to professionalize the force met with the following response, as quoted by a Syracuse policeman in James Q. Wilson's *Varieties of Police Behavior*: ". . . a lot of the men, particularly the older men, had . . . a hard time getting used to the idea of being courteous to the public."[6]

In a recent article in *The New Yorker*, Police Constable Peter Roland Sawyer, of the London Metropolitan Police Force, commented on a few factors that help to explain the discrepancy:

> As far as possible, we want to avoid setting ourselves apart from the public. . . . We're taught enough self-defense so that if a chap comes at you with a missile or an iron bar, you should be able to handle him. . . . I suppose it is possible to imagine a situation in which one would feel justified in drawing the truncheon. Say you were surrounded by a group of real toughs—leather-jacketed chaps swinging bicycle chains. And they wouldn't listen to reason. If you had your back to the wall, your stick would be your last line of defense. I certainly would never draw the truncheon on a crowded street. I think any pro-police feeling that the people had would then become instantly anti. "Look at that big bully," they'd say. No, the police can't have that. We don't want to give ourselves a bad name with the public if we can avoid it. . . . The first aim of a policeman is to take the heat out of the situation. He must do this whether it involves two people or two hundred. His approach is the same—the use of tact and conciliatory methods. He must never show

himself as an authoritarian individual but always as a human being. In many countries, the police rely on sheer weight of numbers and equipment. In this country, we are very thinly policed—about one policeman for every five hundred inhabitants, which I think is the lowest in Europe. New York City has about ten thousand more policemen than London has. Here, we know we've got to keep a tie-in with the public. The English public—they're as good as gold. All you need to do is give them a little guidance.[7]

In the United States there are approximately 40,000 police agencies. Of these, 250 are state and federal. The remainder, roughly 37,500, are agencies of varying sizes representing villages, counties, cities, municipalities, and boroughs. The thought of a national police is foreign to the American temper and inimical to the concept of participatory democracy, which is one of the political ideas on which the nation was founded. The proliferation of small independent police jurisdictions has certainly hindered the formation of a national police. Lately, however, it has not greatly helped to bring about close ties and a sense of mutual respect between police and citizen. Since the citizen played no meaningful role in the development of the police service, it was hard not to create the rigid distinction between amateur and professional or "civilian" and "sworn"; moreover, the departments themselves were anything but participatory democracies. The attempts to introduce technological and bureaucratic systems had the unfortunate side effect of removing the beat patrolman from most, if not all, of his non-law-enforcement contacts with the citizens, thus further increasing the alienation. In addition, bringing us to the present, we have seen within a decade social change greater than our grandfathers experienced in half a century. Now we have an authoritarian, semimilitary police virtually at war with a highly visible segment of the population who are not "criminals" in any useful meaning of that word, although at times they may engage in unlawful behavior.

Earliest efforts to "solve" the problem centered on the creation of special units within police departments, generally known as Police–Community Relations (P–CR) Units. These have been generally ineffectual for a variety of reasons, including resistance of police administrators and middle managers to the changes implied. Often, too, patrolmen were reluctant to accept low-status positions within the police hierarchy on inadequately supported, underfinanced units, carrying few if any professional rewards. With the police identity committed to arrest and apprehension, assignment to service-oriented posts constituted for most officers a removal from real police work. In addition, the communities in question remained suspicious of police intentions, often with justification. Frequently P–CR units were more concerned with adjusting the police image in a community than with improving or broadening the police service the people received.

For these and other reasons, it soon became obvious that the separate P–CR unit was an inadequate response to the problem. Gradually, the best thinking has evolved in the direction of viewing each police officer as a community relations officer. We know that the lowest-ranking patrolman has the greatest contact with the community. In this sense he is at the apex of an inverted pyramid, and at times he must certainly feel that he carries the entire weight load about with him as he performs his job. Police officers who have the least training, the least education, the least amount of power and prestige and reward within the police hierarchy—indeed, within the entire criminal justice system—nevertheless have the greatest discretionary power when it comes to contact with individual members of the public.

Many police administrators, therefore, now believe that police–community relations is the responsibility of the entire force. The problem, of course, is that from top to bottom there is resistance to change, and the view continues to be expressed that "more of the same" will solve the problems. Some, that is, would pump more men, more money, more technology, into a police system that has not kept pace with social change.

In our view, the problems cannot even be properly approached without three specific changes.

1. Police self-image and the public's perception of the police role must be radically altered.
2. There must be a radical increase in citizen involvement and citizen participation in law enforcement.
3. There must be a radical increase, qualitatively and quantitatively, in police skills. This refers both to individual skills, implying training and higher education, and to organizational capacity.

In our estimation, if these changes do not occur, there is little chance that we will be able to fulfill the historic police mission of preserving public order. If they are achieved, sincerely and wholeheartedly, we believe there is a good chance that the present unsatisfactory relationship between police and community can be turned around, becoming one that serves the needs of both.

Police–community relations is nothing more than an attempt to correlate the police operation and community needs; the attempt to develop an environment of community approval for police functions. This is patently impossible so long as the people feel that the police are "essentially beyond their understanding and control."

4. Citizen Participation

It is axiomatic among police that the less citizens have to do with the process of law enforcement the better it is for the police—there is less interference as the police go about their work, less "second-guessing," less "control." The reverse is actually the case. The greater the citizen's involvement and participation in the criminal justice system, the easier it is for the police to request and receive compliance, support, and comfort. Even tangential involvement is better than none. In communities which are hostile and resistant to the police mission and least involved in helping to achieve it, the police experience the most interference, second-guessing, and clamor for citizen "control" of police. Thus the more the community is involved, the better the relationship is going to be between community and police. The better the relationship, the greater the trust, the less the interference. The less interference, the less control. The cry of citizens for control over police simply represents the desire to participate with the police professional in defining crime in the neighborhoods and the nature of the police service the people are to receive. This seems to us to be a completely sensible aim, one that can lead only to increased citizen respect for police efforts.

An illustrative situation occurred during my (J.F.) service in a high-crime area of New York. The city administration had set up regular meetings between representatives of the municipal agencies and members of the community. At these meetings complaints were regularly made about police actions and inaction. High crime rates were a particular sore point with members of minority groups, who lived in the slum neighborhoods and were being subjected to criminal assault on their persons or property. Opinions were voiced that the police were insensitive to the needs of the poor, that they furnished better service to the areas that were occupied by middle- and upper-class residents or commercial and industrial concerns.

Articulate members of the group attending the meetings insisted on having a say about the distribution of personnel and services of the police. One way of convincing them that police services in the area were being properly administered was to invite observation and participation in discussions on police needs and practices. This was done. The police indeed offered to work with a committee along these lines. To refuse to do so would have reinforced the community's idea that the police had something to hide. Arrangements were made for weekly meetings at which the community would be shown how and why police resources were deployed.

After two or three meetings the committee ceased to function. The citizens had found that the police were operating in a fair and efficient manner, and they agreed that further meetings would be held only when conditions warranted it. If their attention had not been welcomed, however, they would not have believed the police had nothing to hide.

Citizen involvement can take many forms. On numerous occasions in American history, *ad hoc* citizen's groups have formed to supplement the police effort or to replace it. A report on the American vigilante tradition submitted to the National Commission on the Causes and Prevention of Violence indicates that instances of people "taking the law into their own hands"—an American tradition that goes back to the South Carolina "Regulators" in the 1760s —predominated in the absence of effective law enforcement in frontier regions.[1] "Vigilante movements were characteristically in the control of the frontier elite and represented their social values and preferences," writes Richard Maxwell Brown.[2] Some hold that the same is also true of the Black Panther party of Oakland, California, which came into being during the 1960s. During the past two centuries more than 300 such citizens' groups have been formed, the more recent ones being mainly black, with the primary purposes of self-patrol and self-protection. Not all such groups have been as hostile to the police as the Black Panthers. Indeed, some have been not hostile at all.

Citizen participation can take many forms in addition to the formation of an *ad hoc* group to patrol the community. Citizen advisory committees have played important roles in maintaining lines of communications with police. The community service officer concept takes selected citizens from the community into the force to serve as an informed and involved liaison between the community and the police. In New York City, selected precincts have hired citizens from the community to greet people coming into the station house. We have found that the people who are involved in this "receptionist" program have developed a better understanding of the role of the police. The program has resulted in an increase in police credibility in the neighborhood, as well. (Citizen involvement is also an effective method of identifying police agencies that are not trying to relate to the community but are merely paying lip service to the concept or are limiting themselves primarily to public relations efforts.)

In the programs mentioned, the participation of the citizen implies above all else an increase in citizen understanding of the criminal justice system: not only how it functions, but what its current grave disabilities and limitations are. From this citizen sophistication, and only from this source, can flow citizen concern capable of producing changes. Then the people will be able to exert pressure on the executives and the legislative bodies of their cities, thus helping create a better criminal justice system. In very large measure, inequities and flaws in the criminal justice system are the result of the community's prior apathy and unconcern. At any rate, too many people who go through the criminal justice system are convinced that games are being played with their lives, and to the extent that the police are identified with such a system, there will be cynicism within the community. Citizen participation in law enforcement is one way of identifying the police as an organization having as a function the protection of the people—all the people—from the inequities of the system of which everyone is a part.

5. Community Service Officers

> One incompetent officer can trigger a riot, perma-
> nently damage the reputation of a citizen, or alien-
> ate a community against a police department.[1]

In these words the President's Commission on Law
Enforcement and Administration of Justice indicated that
inadvertence on the part of the patrolman responding
to a call can cause grievous harm to relations between
the police and the community. In predominantly Spanish-
speaking neighborhoods, for example, it is not uncom-

mon for a citizen who speaks English poorly or not at all to summon the police and then be unable to make himself understood by the responding officer. Less frequently, but often enough to be noted, a policeman confronted by a crowd of people speaking a language he does not understand becomes edgy and arrests the most voluble, excited, or irrational person present. As it happens, this is likely to be the complainant. It does not take many such incidents to turn a neighborhood against the police.

Insofar as the typical minority group community is concerned, a very serious language gap exists, regardless of whether all the participants in an encounter speak English. This gap has to do with emotional language, and the extent to which the police officer is divorced from or distant from the community will tend to determine whether the citizen thinks of the police, and the entire criminal justice system, as "talking another language."

Such alienation can be reduced effectively and with a minimum of administrative and structural disruption by the introduction of Community Service Officers (CSOs) into the police–community equation. The CSO, who is himself a resident of the community, serves basically as an interpreter, either from language to language or from one life condition to another life condition. It is each officer's responsibility to accomplish this goal as well as he can on his own. It is desirable, however, to give him as much help as possible, and this the Community Service Officer is uniquely able to do.

It was, of course, within itself that the community initially found its police officers. Indeed, each member of the community was once expected to donate some time to police duties. It was only when wealthier citizens began to hire others to take their turns in this service function that the idea of a professional officer began to develop.

Until recently, it was against the policy of the New York City Police Department for officers to live in the communities they served. It was felt that this "nonresidence" requirement would remove some of the pressures contributing to corruption, relieve the pressure of being constantly on call, reduce the incidence of harassment due to official actions taken by the officer, and improve his objectivity. Whatever the merits of these arguments, the police officer who in no way belongs to the community is not very likely to take a personal interest in the needs of the community. Thus the introduction of a resident Community Service Officer into the police structure, if it does nothing else, will answer the need for police-type personnel who are involved in the neighborhoods.

The idea of a Community Service Officer was first broached by the President's Commission, which intended the CSO post to fill five primary purposes: to improve the quality of police functioning in high-crime and high-tension neighborhoods, to be a source of empathy and understanding of minority group attitudes and viewpoints, to assume police duties of a purely service nature, to provide minority group members an additional means of gaining entrance to law enforcement work, and to expand and diversify the available pool for police manpower requirements.[2]

The CSO is seldom a sworn, armed member of the police force. In addition to being a resident of the community, he should have personal attributes that the people are likely to value: directness, honesty, a willingness to speak out, strength of character, and evident concern for the welfare of his community. It often happens among minority groups that persons displaying these qualities have a police record. Applicants should be considered (and in fact have been hired, successfully) despite this disability, when an overall appraisal of an individual's character warrants it. Commission studies have indicated that otherwise suitable applicants are difficult to find. For the same reason, strict educational requirements are not desirable.

The typical CSO is young and alert, motivated, very likely, by the desire to do social service work. One black 21-year-old, hired as a CSO in Holyoke, Massachusetts, gave as his motivations curiosity about police work and a strongly felt need to help people. "If it doesn't help the people," he told an interviewer, "I won't do police work." [3]

CSOs do not have full law enforcement powers. Generally their duties consist of aiding the sick or the elderly and performing similar service functions, working with youth, facilitating referral of citizen complaints to social service agencies, assisting police officers in family crisis interventions, and otherwise acting as a buffer between police and community in sensitive matters. In all these functions, the CSO operates as a visible police presence with some of the qualities of a community ombudsman, having been explicitly mandated to serve as a community resource.

The CSO idea has been adopted by a number of cities, and in most instances the programs have been successful in some if not all the aspects named. One of the first cities in the United States to respond to the call for community service officers was Atlanta, Georgia. Chief Herbert Jenkins had been a member of the National Advisory Commission on Civil Disorders, which had not only urged that a CSO program be adopted but had recommended that the federal government support these programs in cities of 50,000 population or more (by reimbursing the police departments 90 percent of the cost of employing one CSO for every ten full-time officers). Federal funds were available in Atlanta, and the program went forward with 50 CSOs; funds were supplied by Atlanta's Mayor Ivan Allen. The CSOs were all previously unemployed residents of the ghetto, and most lacked training. The CSOs wore uniforms but were not issued weapons, and their assignment was to help keep their neighborhoods cool during the anticipated long hot summer of 1968. Chief Jenkins had this to say about the program:

> In most instances, the reason the CSOs were recruited . . . is that they had been involved with the police over some minor violations of the law. By making such a person a CSO, it is hoped this responsibility will curb his unlawful instincts and orient him toward more useful endeavors within an orderly society. . . . We think we have found a way not only to cool off high crime areas but recruit police officers too.[4]

In one small eastern city four CSOs were hired in a mixed neighborhood to accurately reflect its demographic characteristics: two were Spanish-speaking, one was black, and one a French-speaking white. It shortly became evident that in encounters with the police blacks tended to cooperate more readily when the black CSO was present, not because it was in his power to give them a break, but because of their anticipation that they would be treated more fairly. A spokesman for the black community said she believed that a black police officer would not have evoked the same response. This may be partly because the CSO often does not wear the traditional police blues but a "uniform" of blue blazer and grey flannel slacks. But more important, the CSO is identified by the community as an intermediary between itself and the police.

In San Antonio, Texas, the CSOs operate from within

the department's Community Relations Bureau, which is headed by a captain and consists of nine police officers, ten civilian community service officers, and one secretary. The CSOs, who are chosen from the population of the city's federal housing projects, maintain field headquarters (Community Service Offices) from which they make referrals for jobs, welfare benefits, and education and health services; organize recreational activities; and provide liaison and educational functions between police and area citizens.

In Worcester, Massachusetts, in addition to the aforementioned duties, the CSOs report and locate stolen cars and receive complaints concerning abandoned cars, unsanitary conditions, or minor neighborhood disturbances.

One of the most ambitious CSO projects has been instituted in Chicago, where there are 422 Community Service Aides. In conjunction with foot patrolmen, the aides create a combined resident–police patrol team that allows the police department to maintain meaningful contact with the people of the community, thus helping reduce crime in high-crime areas. Chicago's CSAs are being utilized in four Model City neighborhoods. They operate out of six storefront Community Service Centers. Each center is open 12 to 14 hours daily, under the command of a police lieutenant who has up to 100 CSAs at his disposal, in addition to the sergeants and patrolmen. The basic team of one patrolman and seven to seventeen aides patrols the beat on foot. Their contacts with the community are predominantly nonauthoritarian. Emphasis is on service functions, including protecting school children at crossings; helping with traffic at athletic events; supervising playgrounds and libraries; clearing the streets of junk cars; reporting sanitation violations and other forms of environmental pollution; and reporting sick persons, lost children, and dangerous and hazardous conditions. The aides also act as receptionists in police stations.

The emphasis on nonregulatory foot patrols is clearly an attempt to restore human contact and recognition between the police and the community, for it is the loss of this relationship in a time of rapid urban change—and with police moving toward increasingly mechanized patrol—that has exacerbated police–community conflicts. Unlike programs emphasizing the CSOs' "civilianness," the Chicago program puts the aides in uniform to serve as a conspicuous reminder of the police presence. The aides, however, do not make arrests (nor do they work in detention facilities, make case reports on crime, drive Department vehicles, or work in building maintenance), and they are primarily service oriented. They are concerned with the general welfare of the community, and to get that message across they frequently make house-to-house visits to identify themselves and to invite residents of the neighborhood to come to the Community Service Centers and make known their complaints about police service.

The most significant structural feature of the Chicago program is the amount of training the aides receive. Because of it, the CSA program truly provides an apprenticeship for law-enforcement jobs. It is expected that some though not many of the CSAs will go on to become police officers. Others, barred by rigid height or other physical requirements, will doubtless be sought by private industry as guards, watchmen, and security officers.

The training program is divided into three phases. The first two phases consist of 200 hours of in-service training in such subjects as Criminal Law Administration, Department Standards, Field Procedures, Investigation, Social Sciences, and Management Development. Phase three

consists of 55 hours of advanced work in the same subjects. In addition, CSAs are encouraged to continue their
formal education, and aides can be excused from duty,
for a maximum of nine hours a week, to attend classes
leading a high-school diploma or a college degree.

The Community Service Bureau in the Chicago Police
Department is particularly enthusiastic about its aide
program. Many of the young people involved, formerly
high-school dropouts, have resumed their education and
received diplomas, and some have gone on to do college-
level work. In the 21st District, where 42 aides have been
hired, 17 are enrolled in city colleges. The hope is that
these young men and women will *not* make a career in
the CSA program but that they will be motivated to continue their education to become equipped for employment
at good wages in the private sector.

In this way the CSA program, in addition to supporting
pragmatic police goals for improved service and better
community relations, acts as a supplemental corrections
and rehabilitation program. Therefore, it is particularly
important that departments remain flexible in setting
standards of acceptability for applicants to CSO programs, notably by not excluding applicants with prior
police records for minor offenses. The program offers
young people perhaps their only chance to gain stability
in an unstable environment and to overcome the influ-
ences that led to their previous destructive and antisocial
behavior. This highly beneficial side effect can be obtained
even if the program does not have the goal explicitly
stated, or even intended. A program of this nature, on a
small scale, has been operating effectively in Mount
Vernon, New York, and coordinator William Wetteroth
feels the aides are doing a very creditable job.

One word of caution is needed here. It is extremely

important that any CSO program be kept from degenerating into a sloppily administered or poorly supervised operation. On the one hand, the CSOs' credibility in the community must not be impaired, as it surely will be if the program does not have the continuing support and interest of the administrators and supervisors. On the other hand, the aides themselves need to feel that they are making a real contribution to the ongoing public safety effort in their community. Without a purpose, they will swiftly become bored, very likely falling into careless and irresponsible behavior. If this should happen, it is important that the boredom, frustration, and listlessness parallel the inefficiency and waste of bureaucratic functioning (which can overtake a police department as well as any other hierarchical organization). Such negative qualities that mirror a badly run bureaucracy may be produced by it as well.

For the same reasons, it continues to be important that police officers working with CSOs be volunteers. No program of this nature is going to work unless the individual officers are committed to it. In time, a body of evidence will accumulate to prove the value of such programs to even their most intractable or bigoted opponents; but in the meantime, no one should be forced to participate.

In Chicago, as in other cities, there is a large stack of pending applications by police officers very much interested in becoming part of this program. Not all policemen, however, are willing to recognize that the young minority group citizen, functioning as a community service officer, is an ally and partner of inestimable value in the work of crime prevention and crime control. Yet eventually most will see the light, and when that day comes, it will be a critical and noteworthy moment in the evolution of police work.

6. Youth Patrols

Despite certain obvious similarities, youth patrols differ from community service officer programs in significant ways, the most important being that youth patrols are outside the police hierarchy and have not been formed by, or perhaps even welcomed by, the police. The CSO is of the police as well as of the neighborhood; the youth patrol is only of the neighborhood.

Most youth patrols are formed as a response to crisis.

When the crisis subsides, they tend to lose impetus and disintegrate. In addition, the participants cooperate with the police as a pragmatic gesture but often they are anti-police in orientation. Some, like the Black Panthers in Oakland, were formed specifically to monitor police patrol activities. A decade earlier, a self-defense patrol of blacks in Monroe, North Carolina, repelled with gunfire an attack by the Ku Klux Klan on the home of one of its members. Terry Ann Knopf writes:

> The earlier youth patrols shared a number of characteristics. In virtually every case, the members were young and were recruited from within the black community; some had previous records of arrest. In addition, they shared a common belief that it was their community and that they bore a responsibility for its welfare. To a great extent, their basic assumptions about the need for such groups were negative: that the white community was hostile and could not be trusted; that the civil authorities were mere extensions of the white community and could not be expected to act fairly; and that the local police were to be especially feared since they had the instruments of power more readily at their disposal and could (and did) harm instead of protect the black community. Consequently, in Monroe, a "self defense guard" was created to protect the community *against* the Klan; in Watts, a Community Alert Patrol was formed to act as a *buffer* between the police and the black community; and, in Oakland, the Black Panther Party for Self-Defense was established "to preserve the community from harm" *by the police*. Most of these groups operated independently of the police and other civil authorities. Relations between the two groups were largely characterized by a high degree of suspicion on both sides.[1]

It goes without saying that any community feeling the need to create a citizen's patrol to protect it from the police is suffering from poor police–community relations. However, police need not always fear and resist these units. Sometimes relations between the community and the police have improved following the formation of such a patrol. At any rate, the work they do has been of vital assistance to the police. In the Watts section of Los Angeles in 1966, for example, the Community Alert Patrol was praised by the police for its work patrolling the Watts Summer Festival, and most other youth patrols have been praised by mayors, police chiefs, or other city officers. A captain on the Grand Rapids, Michigan, police department said of the city's youth patrol, "They're doing a beautiful job. And, believe me, we appreciate it."

The extent to which a police department will welcome (or perhaps even encourage) a citizens' patrol varies with local circumstances. Generally speaking, youth patrols have come into existence as a response to rioting in the community—a number, for example, were formed during the turmoil following the assassination of Dr. Martin Luther King, Jr. Not infrequently there was the implicit assumption that additional police activities would exacerbate rather than soothe the community disturbances. Some police departments are unwilling to recognize that the uniformed policeman often symbolizes to the minority group member a complex of social injustices not of the officer's making. These departments tend to react defensively to the suggestion that a strong show of police presence is not necessarily the best way to achieve public tranquillity. A low police profile is sometimes advisable, but the short-sighted view is not uncommon. It has been summed up in the phrases of a police administrator who complained, "Are we always going to have to conform to their ways? Isn't this a two-way street? Don't they have to conform to our ways?" The answer, of course, is that the primary issue is not the propriety—or lack of it—of any one's "ways," but the skill and understanding and flexibility with which the police perform their function. When any device—such as youth patrols—serves to lessen or eliminate community disorder, police should think carefully before rejecting it.

The Lemberg Center for the Study of Violence at Brandeis University has investigated the operation of youth patrols in a number of cities and has determined that in more than 75 percent of the cases, their appearance on the street "coincided with either a reduction or virtual cessation of violence." [2] This statistic takes on greater significance when we consider that the youth patrols in question consisted of untrained youngsters in their late teens or early twenties, who voluntarily gathered together in the midst of civil disorder to help restore calm. In Boston the Youth Alliance Security Patrol distributed the following flyer:

> Cool it. The riot squad has M-16's, Stoner rifles, MACE, a machine so high-pitched it will make you deaf. They're not playing. Keep off the streets. Defend your home and family, but don't start anything. Cool it. [3]

In some cases, patrol members themselves had been rioters, yet they were no less effective for that, because the primary weapon at the disposal of the youth patrols (not being authorized to bear weapons or to coerce public behavior) is persuasion—a device for achieving compliance that is effective in proportion to the persuader's personal credibility and authority. In Boston, in Providence, and in Grand Rapids, youth patrols faced angry, hostile crowds and managed to defuse the situation sufficiently to avert violence.

Youth patrols, incidentally, are not the same as auxiliaries, which are much more formal than the youth or citizen patrols. An auxiliary patrol has been trained by the police, membership qualifications have been defined by police regulations, and the police assume complete responsibility for the unit's operations. Auxiliaries are a useful adjunct to the police, particularly for nonenforcement duties or for patrol in low-crime areas, subway patrol, park patrol, church synagogue patrol, and so forth. The presence of a uniformed though generally unarmed auxiliary is reassuring to citizens. And certainly auxiliaries can serve very effectively as aides in crowd control, especially when many people attend peaceful demonstrations and athletic or recreational events.

In operation, auxiliaries have varied slightly from city to city. In Philadelphia there are three officer levels (captain, lieutenant, sergeant), which are used for all disturbances except labor disturbances. When in uniform and on duty, the members are authorized to make arrests. In Flint, Michigan, the auxiliary function is informal and voluntary. Fort Worth, Texas, has an auxiliary force of 75 men working at night, doing regular patrol work in one-man cars. In Houston, boys of 19 are full-fledged members, sworn, uniformed, and armed, with unlimited arrest powers, after three months of training.

In Los Angeles a Reserve Corps is made up of dedicated citizens who conform closely to police requirements, pass written examinations, and are trained, uniformed, and equipped like regular members of the force. Unpaid except for a small stipend for expenses incurred while on duty, the reservists perform at least two tours of duty each month. They may be assigned to any phase of police work, including radio motor patrol.

In 1968 the New York City Police Department derived some beneficial service and satisfactory experience from youth patrols in a few areas of the city. In sensitive areas, a group of young people were hired to act as community liaison personnel to keep city agencies aware of incipient problems. Local police commanders, among others, were asked to recommend individuals who were representative of neighborhood groups and could be effective in molding youth opinion and behavior.

The city had enlisted this corps of young people during the presummer quietude, hoping to have available, in the rather likely event of civil disorder, some people of the community who could go to the scene and command a certain amount of personal authority. Since unemployment was high and it was known that there would be a lot of young people on the street and at loose ends, gang leaders, club leaders, and other young men who could be presumed to be influential in their neighborhoods were contacted. Very often we found that those who were most qualified were those who had been in trouble with the police earlier.

Of course the individuals chosen were not people who would have allowed themselves to become police shills, and this suited police needs perfectly. We wanted this body of community opinion-makers to persuade their peers that their needs and the community's needs were not necessarily best served by violent acts and that the solution to local problems did not necessarily lie in hostile and aggressive behavior.

In another instance, Mobilization For Youth (an organization founded in 1962 and financed by federal, city, and private funds) formed a group, some of whose members had police records. Created for nonenforcement police duties, this patrol was not given sufficient attention by the police; therefore, it did nothing to prevent or cool down a riot at Avenue C and 9th Street, the so-called East Village, in the summer of 1969. Subsequently, MFY took the patrol members off the police run and assigned them to fire duty. They were given white helmets and put to work with the Fire Department, which was then experiencing a considerable amount of community hostility during fire-fighting runs. The youth patrol was equipped with radio apparatus so that it could receive fire alarms. Youth patrol members responding to alarms in private cars provided by the mayor's office helped direct traffic, establish fire lanes, and otherwise prevent interference with the fire-fighting effort.

An earlier youth patrol effort had been organized in the East Village when friction and violence developed between minority group residents and hippie youth who invaded the area in 1967. Local youth—black, white, and Puerto Rican—identified by white armbands, circulated through Tomkins Square Park during concerts, dances, and other recreational events to keep peace among the spectators who maintained conflicting life styles. The members of this patrol were called "Serenos"— the Spanish word for watchman or peace-keeper.

The sucessful examples just cited notwithstanding, the formation of youth patrols raises certain problems. The most important one is the characteristic disinclination of many policemen to support the patrols—partly due to the implication that the presence of youth patrols is somehow indicative of police failure to do their job properly. The police, in fact, may not be doing their job properly if they fail to utilize youth patrols under certain circumstances.

For their part, the youth patrol members are grievously subject to boredom once the crisis that motivated their participation has passed. Sometimes this manifests itself in a high personnel turnover rate, sometimes in an increased desire for the trappings of authority, such as a nightstick or handcuffs. The members of such patrols, remember, tend to be active, resourceful individuals who possess leadership attributes. Such persons will not happily allow their scope to be limited, and they are swiftly frustrated by bureaucratic regulations, inefficiency, or an apparent lack of cooperation. If, for example, their reports of abandoned cars, abandoned refrigerators, and unhealthy or unsanitary conditions are ignored, they will conclude that they are being used and exploited and will soon quit. It is a very serious error to involve young people as volunteers with the law enforcement effort and through carelessness, inadvertence, ineptitude, or cynicism allow them to become disillusioned. It would have been better by far not to have sought their participation in the first place.

Even if youth patrol programs are effective during crisis —as they frequently seem to have been—the communities are sufficiently sophisticated to observe that none of their real and continuing problems are being attended to, and police are still perceived as apologists who are buying time or pouring oil on troubled waters. To the extent that youth patrols partake of this identification, their value to the police is compromised.

The *ad hoc* youth patrol, formed to combat a specific crisis situation and discontinued when the critical time has passed, has the greatest value both during the time of its operation and afterward, in memory. Most important for the members of the patrol is the knowledge that they have not been in any way coopted into even the semblance of defending the power structure; thus their credibility in the community remains unimpaired. For their part, the police do not have to face the problems attendant on keeping a group of high-spirited young men enthusiastic about increasingly prosaic and unglamorous chores. This, we should add parenthetically, is a problem police administrators will face increasingly as they recruit better-educated men into the department.

7. Against Discord

In former years it was primarily the hardened criminal with whom the police came into contact. The person we recall with fondness and nostalgia as "the law-abiding citizen" encountered the police, if at all, in connection with minor traffic violations. More recently, this idealized John Q. Public figure has allowed his hair to grow, has come to question national policy, and has begun to protest and demonstrate against long-established public institutions—or for peace, student rights, or women's rights.

And no broad consensus has yet developed about how this behavior should be handled.

Certainly a considerable segment of the public feels that protestors should be handled firmly, if not roughly, and packed off to jail. This attitude found its ultimate expression in the words of a woman in Kent, Ohio, who said after the Kent State tragedy of May 1970, that students who demonstrated *should* be shot. This is a horrible and yet perfectly logical extension of the principle that disruption of public order can be successfully dealt with entirely, or primarily, as a distinct phenomenon apart from all related factors, through an authoritarian display of power. A large segment of the population found the events at Kent State to be a particularly repugnant display of the state's power to resist citizens' legitimate right to assemble. Some wished the students indicted; others wished the National Guard indicted. Unfortunately, such a confused condition is transmitted to the police as conflicting, in some cases irreconcilable, demands from the public. The police organization needs to divorce itself as much as possible from the complex moral questions having to do with resistance to change. This they have not fully done, although their current attitude is better than it was during the rise of the labor union movement.

Until the past decade, there had been no significant expressions of civil unrest in the United States since the labor agitation early in the century. The benefits that organized labor brought to the American working people—together with the unifying experience of World War II—kept the nation together until the disintegrating 1960s. The catalyst for the change of the national fiber was, of course, the Negro revolution early in the decade—a revolution that can be said to have begun when one woman resolutely refused to go to the back of the bus.

This social transformation, which turned "Negroes" into "blacks," differed only in details from the equally disruptive upheaval that earlier had turned the lower classes into working men and women with meaningful economic power. It is ironic and disturbing (and probably inevitable) that the greatest resistance to the desire of black people for social and economic parity comes largely from the very people who fear that they may not be able to consolidate their gains.

In the United States, of course, the idea of the right to resist authority perceived as illegitimate or unreasoning is very firmly rooted. Indeed the founding of the nation depended on that very principle. Consequently, we should not wonder at the disintegrating decade we have only recently passed through—with riots in the cities, half a nation against a war the other half of the nation supported, and a generation of children discarding as they grow up many of the social and sexual attitudes their elders held dear. "Our nation was born of civil dissatisfaction and dissent," said Patrick V. Murphy at the Third Institute on the Criminal Justice System, at the New York Police Academy on October 6, 1971. "It is our heritage." [1]

What has been notable about this period is the intensity and the rate of change. Few people and none of our institutions were prepared to cope with it:

> Law enforcement in particular immediately embarked upon "crash programs" for sorely needed and thoroughly overdue community relations programs, disorder prevention studies and crowd control training. Our efforts have borne fruit. We have progressed to where we are much better equipped to control mass population problems today. But there are still questions awaiting answers. Have we progressed far enough? Have we prepared ourselves properly for the future? My response to

these queries must be in the negative. . . . I have
said and will continue to say that more imaginative
and innovative changes must be forthcoming.[2]

In our view, the area of civilian participation stands as
the greatest source, and potentially the most useful
source, of imagination and innovation in the police mission. Here, where such police traits as clannishness,
secrecy, and defensiveness are likely to lead to resistance
of any civilian involvement, lies the greatest possibility
for altering the present arrangement, where the policeman is essentially an alienated authoritarian (parent) figure and the public is potentially the guilty or at any
rate suspicious-seeming (child) figure. Each succeeding
police–citizen contact that is not within that self-defeating
dialogue but is mutually supportive, helps to tear down
the wall that has grown up between the people and their
police.

One meaningful step in the right direction was taken
in the Precinct Receptionist Program—New York City's
previously mentioned experiment in which women of the
community were hired as receptionists at station houses.
This meant that the citizen, entering the station house,
encountered a friendly and cooperative figure whose purpose was to give aid.

The Annual Report of the Office of the Deputy Commissioner for Community Relations described the program
in the following manner:

In the interest of increasing its capacity to assist
persons troubled with non-police problems, those
requiring referral to social service agencies or other
city departments, the Police Department instituted
the Precinct Receptionist Program.
Begun as a volunteer program in the 23rd Precinct,

located in East Harlem, the project placed mature, respected women from the local community in the station house to act as both receptionists and interpreters. . . . The Receptionist's duties include interviewing the person seeking help, in order to determine what the problem is and what services are available to meet it. Then, using specially prepared information directories and other resources, the Receptionist locates an appropriate service agency to assist the troubled person and puts the person into immediate contact with the helping agency.

In May of 1968, the Department received a grant of $167,800.00 from the Ford Foundation for the extension and development of the Precinct Receptionist Program on a salaried basis. This grant also enabled the Department to a hire a professional, administrative staff, consisting of a Project Director, two Referral Consultants and an Executive Assistant. In addition to administering the program, they recruit Receptionists in coordination with the Precinct Commanding Officer, train and supervise the Receptionists. On all tours of duty a Referral Consultant is available via telephone or in person, to answer the receptionist's questions and recommend an appropriate course of action in any situation. The grant will also provide for a study of the project, with regard to incorporating it into the formal structure of the Police Department. The professional staff works closely with the Police Department and community organizations in an effort to expand the services of the Receptionist program.[3]

This receptionist program, which utilizes the services of females exclusively, suggests a few words on women in police. Clearly a police increasingly oriented toward service needs to reappraise its attitudes to women, perhaps beginning to discard traditional prejudices. There is a growing need for women to handle nonenforcement police work, and we do not by any means refer only to clerical jobs. The female sensibility can calm contentious individuals, and there is no reason why certain types of community discord could not be managed as well by female professionals in conflict management as by male professionals. Female community service officers have been found to be as effective as males in the Chicago and Mount Vernon CSO programs. And, of course, women have an established role in juvenile and vice work. We have in mind, however, the possibility of even more radical approaches, including male–female patrol teams with special responsibilities, let us say, in family conflict management. This whole area cries out for innovative programming. In some urban areas women are on patrol duty.

Among the cities that have begun to explore new uses for civilians in police work is Omaha, Nebraska. This midwestern city has developed a program wherein civilians are enabled to direct traffic and issue citations for stationary automobile violations. According to Public Safety Director Al Pattavina, this has involved creating the new position of traffic controller—a citizen not as well trained as a policeman, somewhat lower salaried, and unarmed. It is Pattavina's view, and ours, that improved police–community relations require structural innovation and "will not just naturally follow from pleasant discussions between the upper echelons of leadership in police departments and community organizations." [4]

We do not mean to undervalue pleasant discussions between any echelon of police and community. By far the most depressing statistic to come out of police-attitude studies is the one revealing that police think people are more antipolice than they actually are. Indicating as this does not only an unnecessarily poor police self-image but a vast distortion of perception, it suggests even more urgently the need for increased police–citizen contact of every conceivable kind.

To this end a number of cities have instituted a wide variety of contact programs—some pragmatic and job-related, others consisting of dialogue encounters. Washington, D. C., has a "React" project in which private citizens with ham radios in their cars patrol three high-crime precincts on weekends, transmitting information to a base station that relays it to a police dispatcher. In Kansas City, Missouri, there is an emergency alert program called "Operation Barrier," which involves taxi, trucking, and public-utility firms. More than 700 radio-equipped vehicles function as an information network linked by direct telephone lines to the police through agency dispatchers.

Newport News, Virginia, has a Block Mother Program. Participating women put signs in their windows identifying themselves as available to help young children in need. (In a more cohesive community, this service would of course be intrinsically provided.) In Los Angeles, teenagers are hired as junior police and perform clerical duties within the department. The buddy system established in Elizabeth, New Jersey, sends 140 teams of matched police and ghetto residents out to patrol the precincts. New York holds police–youth dialogues at summer encampments. Dade County, Florida, makes available officers with a minimum of 10 years of police experience to join high school counselling teams.

In many cities there are regular meetings between police and business and professional people, or between police and students. In one desirable extension of this idea, a fraternity at the University of Nebraska has developed a "Feed the Fuzz" program designed to "try to disestablish the common concept students have of police as head-beating, club-swinging ogres." [5]

In short, anything that gives exposure of police personnel and activities to young people, and vice versa, is likely to be valuable, for it helps to break down the isolation that reinforces stereotypic thinking and intensifies in police and citizen alike a natural fear of what is foreign or strange in one's midst. At one time I (J.F.) approached the Lower East Side Action Project (LEAP), which had a school in operation, and offered the tutorial services of some of the officers of my precinct. After consultation with the program directors, it was decided to use the men to operate a sports clinic. We had a former professional wrestler, a former professional boxer, and a former state weight-lifting champion, among others. We later noted, as a measure of the venture's success, that some of the boys who had formerly given catcalls or used abusive language as radio cars went by began running over to greet the officers on patrol. We experienced a tremendous amount of attitudinal change on the part of the LEAP youngsters, who were considered to be disciplinary problems, and also on the part of the director of the school, who had been a constant critic of the police and who subsequently wrote the police commissioner describing his altered attitude. Involvement with citizens is a step not toward handcuffing the police but toward demolishing discordant relationships between the police and the public.

Even if the fears of criticism and of being misunderstood were as justified as some police administrators believe (though they are not), programs like those mentioned invariably have a mediating effect and lead in the direction of increased civilian understanding and sympathy. The same is true of programs like New York City's annual citywide Police–Clergy Conferences and the quarterly precinct-level police–clergy dialogues. The same is true, in fact, of all programs having as their end result (if not their goal) increased contact and dialogue between the people and the police. The police–clergy precinct meetings, though of limited value, clearly help to build an ongoing relationship with the clergy on a year-round basis. The clergy can play a major role in the police–community dialogue primarily because they are held in esteem and exert influence among their parishioners. In our experience, the clergy have participated in crisis situations on an *ad hoc* basis, with particularly soothing effect on frayed tempers.

The role that business and industry have to play is no less meaningful. In recognition of the complex factors that contribute to criminal activity or antisocial attitudes— among which chronic underemployment for minority youths must be ranked near the top of the list—the police in one New York precinct mounted Operation Job. Police canvassed the merchants of the area for employment opportunities for hard-core unemployables, that is, people who because of a criminal record are unable to secure employment in any but the worst-paid, least-desirable jobs. On the advice of the police, small businessmen will give some people an opportunity for constructive rehabilitation. Other programs of this type, such as one instituted by the Morgan Guaranty Trust and The Delehanty Institute, provided minority group youths with training courses leading to careers in civil service.

More important, perhaps, than the role business can play in offering jobs or funding for experimental programs is the effect that business has on the climate of the precinct. If it is known (or assumed) that local business reaps excessive profits without any compensatory return to the community, the business sector in many instances can be considered to be a source of poor police–community relations. For example, although a person who throws a brick through a grocery store window is liable for arrest, a grocery store owner who creates hostility in a community by overpricing is not. Nor is the slumlord, except very indirectly, through the Health Department or the Buildings Department. Anything that the business community does to express interest, concern, and involvement in the community is positive. There is a furniture store in Harlem, for example, which through the years has helped sponsor various neighborhood police-organized athletic teams. This somewhat indirect involvement by the civilian community in police affairs has a salutary effect on the ability of the police to function.

The role of the police in this instance is to promote within the precinct the greatest possible sense of community. The more cohesive the community, the greater its commitment to shared goals, the more it involves itself in police affairs, and the easier the job of the police. Such involvement is not easily achieved, and part of the police problem is to find a means of showing the citizen that the solution of common problems requires closer cooperation with the police.

Naturally, the police are not going to get this cooperation without first identifying themselves with the community's needs—even becoming catalysts for change, if need be. Many of the conditions that create problems in communities stem from a variety of issues and circumstances that are beyond the immediate remedy of the police agency. Nevertheless, the police, as a 24-hour community resource, are particularly well suited to identify such trouble spots and bring them to the attention of the appropriate public officials or neighborhood councils. The police can act with special effect, for example, in response to community needs for referral. If someone comes to the police to complain of a rat-infested house, he is most likely to be told to notify the Health Department. But suppose the police "take the case" and bring the Health Department on the scene? If a citizen complains about sharp business practices of a merchant, or illegal credit operations, the police will very likely direct him to the Better Business Bureau, or some other appropriate agency. But suppose they "take the case" and lodge a complaint on behalf of John Jones with the local department of consumer affairs?

Is this going beyond current understanding of police responsibilties in this area? Yes, it is, to some extent, but it is not nearly so radical a departure as one would suppose. In some programs now in operation, police are empowered to make direct referrals, to pick people up in radio cars and take them to a destination if such transportation seems to be in the best interest of the community. We are suggesting that an important and meaningful way for the police to increase their belongingness in the communities they serve involves identifying and dealing with social conditions and circumstances that adversely affect a community.

Our own years of experience have left little doubt in our minds that a significant part of the ability to do an effective police job depends on a good relationship with the community, although frequently there is no community with whom to have a good relationship unless police make a point of reaching out. The communities are not necessarily uninterested or even uncooperative. They simply exist in a formless and uncohesive condition. We found that we had to go to the people to urge them to understand the problems and to identify the areas in which they could work with us to achieve a joint objective—whether the goal was as specific as getting street lights up on dangerous corners or as general as dealing with the narcotics situation in the neighborhood. Invariably, working with the community made the police job easier to do.

A dramatic example of the involvement of the police in the social life of the community took place in Waycross, Georgia, when Chief Ray Pope called in community business leaders and told them that racial integration was coming and they were going to get it, whether they tried to forestall it with demonstrations, sit-ins, boycotts, and other disruptive social agitation, or whether they simply desegregated quietly and peacefully. The community leaders saw the logic of Chief Pope's analysis, and they chose the second, peaceful alternative.

Thus far we have been commenting on improved dialogue between police and community based on an increased police involvement in community problems. We have also stressed the increased citizen role that can be played within the police structure. Yet there is a third element, less programmatic and less rigidly organized, that is perhaps equally important: increased visibility of police functioning. Included in this category would be ride-along programs, demonstration observers, and other civilian observer programs proving the police willingness to give up secrecy.

In some precincts of New York City, citizens selected from block associations, tenant groups, and other community organizations ride in police radio cars for two-hour tours. Approximately 40 volunteers—men and women, black and white and Puerto Rican—sit in the back of a patrol car each month to get a firsthand view of police work. Those who participate sign waivers of responsibility, and are also asked not to speak to arrested persons or in any way interfere with the policeman's performance of duty. Impressions of the observers have usually been supportive of and sympathetic to the police. Despite this generally favorable reaction, however, the precinct commander acknowledges that his officers are not wholeheartedly enthusiastic about the program. "After working alone for many years they might be a bit uncomfortable suddenly having a civilian observer in the back seat," he reports. The officers find it difficult to shrug off the fear that the citizens are "spying on them or second-guessing them." [6]

The New York program stresses increased citizen appreciation of police work; others emphasize precisely what the New York policemen fear—the attempt to evaluate the work the police are doing. In Waco, Texas, for example, Baylor Law School students ride in patrol cars. The ride-along program in Omaha also envisions that the civilian volunteers will be making judgments about how the police perform their job; but that is not, according to Deputy Chief Monroe Coleman, a reason to fear it. He expects that the program will not only serve to improve citizen understanding of police work but will possibly improve the quality of the performance: "When you know you are being looked at, hopefully you will perform better." [7]

On the other hand, in Covina, California, "any citizen who registers a complaint against the police department is invited to ride for one evening in a patrol car with officers to see the problems of those concerned with law enforcement." [8]

In New York, a more highly structured variation on civilian observation of police activities has enlisted the services of community leaders within a Civilian Observer Corps. This group oversees disorders and confrontations and conveys information to the local community, to the city government, and to the police. The observers accompany police to the scene of public disturbances and subsequently report to the community on the use (or lack of use) of excessive force. Since the individuals who partici-pate are community leaders with high credibility, their presence frequently neutralizes unsubstantiated charges of police brutality. Most recently, a program has been initiated with the local bar association to provide lawyers as observers.

During mass disorders it is sometimes difficult for police administrators to monitor the situation adequately. In the midst of a melee they may not see what is happening, although afterward they see the results. In such situations, citizen observers serve two functions. Besides making credible reports, they tend to affect the conduct of those involved in the event. The presence of observers does inhibit inappropriate actions by both the police and the protesters.

Perhaps someday a substitute for civilian observers may be found in advanced technology and the use of film and videotape. Where a record exists, circumstances can be evaluated, and blame, if there is any, can properly be fixed. However, photos taken by a police videotape unit are not likely to have the community credibility that a presumably impartial citizens' group would have. The police willingness to cooperate with an observer corps suggests police responsiveness to community review of its work—this in itself is a powerful inducement to better relations.

8. Community Councils

Basically, the police enforce the law and offer equal service to all. That is the principle of law and community contract which binds the people and their police amicably. Most police problems of community hostility or antipathy spring from violations of these principles by the police, or the belief among certain segments of the community that such precepts have been violated, or the inability of certain segments of the community to trust the police intention.

"For the urban poor," writes Michael Harrington in *The Other America*, "the police are those who arrest you. In almost any slum there is a vast conspiracy against the forces of law and order. If someone approaches asking for a person, no one there will have heard of him, even if he lives next door." [1]

Undoubtedly some communities will continue to uphold this wall of intransigence in the face of police efforts to develop better police–community relations. These are times of stress in society and in the body politic. It would be unrealistic to believe that the best efforts of a well-intentioned police administrator are always going to be successful, or even welcomed in the spirit in which they are offered. Nevertheless, it would be wrong and self-defeating to assume that all, most, or even a substantial segment in a community of the poor, the disadvantaged, or the socially and politically alienated will fail to respond to honest police efforts to enforce the law evenhandedly and humanely. A sensitive awareness that the purpose of the law is to maintain community peace and tranquillity with equity and justice will, eventually, be recognized.

It is by now thoroughly comprehended that the people living in high-crime, poverty areas want not less but *more* police service. They do not, however, want the police service they have become accustomed to getting. The education of a patrolman, which begins in the Police Academy, does not end there. It continues during every tour of duty he performs, and the lessons he learns in the street often do not coincide with the best principles of the academy. "For his own good," the recruit is warned by the older officers that he can survive only if he makes everyone on the street understand that "he's the boss." In an urban, high-hazard precinct, the impulse to reduce anxiety by a show of authoritarian presence is well-nigh irresistible to a young, inexperienced patrolman, especially when his peers—and notably the more experienced among them—suggest that this is his strongest weapon. However, the authoritarian policeman wields a two-edged sword: all too often, his actions provoke resistance and anger that might have lain dormant and create overt hostility where it did not previously exist. The policeman's most valuable weapon is widespread recognition and belief that he is there to serve the community's best interest. Obviously, then, a police administrator should attempt to learn how the people of his community perceive their own interests and how they think those interests can best be served.

Col. Robert M. Igleburger, Director of Police, Dayton, Ohio, has observed:

> If crime is of concern to a neighborhood, so are the methods utilized by police departments to combat that crime. While placement of a police officer on every street corner may drastically reduce street crime, it is neither economically nor politically acceptable to do so if for no other reason than that the result would be an army of occupation in a democratic society.[2]

During the latter part of 1968, Dayton attempted to reduce street crime through an increase in preventive patrol activity by police officers in cruisers. An evaluation of the program indicated that the lowering of the incidence of street crime was balanced by a rise in property crimes, such as residential burglaries; in any case, the effect was temporary. According to Igleburger:

> It became obvious that the new preventive patrol methods were not affecting this type of crime. But

more important, the relationship between the police
department and some segments of the community
deteriorated for, while preventive patrol may have
been successful in controlling some crime, it became aggravating to citizens of poor neighborhoods
whose life-styles the police did not completely
understand. Offensive police actions were often
seen by neighborhood residents as repression and
oppression rather than protection.[3]

In the summer of 1966 I (J.F.) was assigned to take command of the Ninth Precinct on the Lower East Side of New
York, which contained a high-density, high-tension population of more than 100,000 people—about 45 percent
Puerto Rican; 40 percent low-income whites of Slavic,
Italian, Jewish, and other backgrounds; and about 15
percent black. Relations between the police and the
community had deteriorated badly. Social service organizations frankly voiced their lack of confidence in the
police. The Lower East Side Action Project, the Young
Adults Action Group, and the Mobilization for Youth—all
concerned with poverty, discrimination, unemployment,
and police abuse of power—frequently found themselves
in confrontation with the police. Little wonder, then, that
the residents of the area saw the police as antagonists
rather than the protectors of their rights and liberty.

At high-level briefings, my introduction to the Ninth
Precinct was focused on the history of the neighborhood
discord; it stressed the importance of establishing a better
relationship with community elements. The first order of
business was to determine exactly how the community
felt about the police—not a simple task. To begin, there
is the difficulty of determining which "leaders" speak only
for themselves and which for a real segment of the community; which voice a programmatic antipolice bias and

which are identifying true flaws in police operations (e.g., brutal policemen) which the police agree ought to be corrected. Next there is the even more difficult problem of creating a forum that is task oriented, pragmatic, and functional. The formation of a precinct council or a police–community relations council does not in itself solve any problems. It can just as easily create some—for example, when the forum is used simply to air hostile feelings between the police and the community. Alternatively, such a citizens' committee, functioning with the personnel in the police–community relations cadre, can just as easily turn into a clubby, polite body that does not represent the true climate of the neighborhood.

In the Ninth Precinct we initiated a series of visits to the directors of community agencies, who were eager to join the police commander in the task of defining community problems and seeking their solutions. We saw easily enough that the primary source of disaffection for the police of the precinct lay in the charge, made repeatedly, that dealing with the police was an adversative procedure—the local residents would deliver charges and the police would return routine defensive responses. Since investigations were either delayed endlessly or forgotten altogether, people deduced that the police did not really want the community's cooperation but only its compliance. Spokesmen indicated that the community was frustrated and resentful; they wanted it known that although they were poor and "disadvantaged," they were human beings entitled to courteous, efficient, and respectful police service.

Among the worthwhile programs that evolved from the meetings was the Grass-Roots Leaders' Conference, which was composed of community representatives from storefront clubs, churches, and ethnic associations, as

well as representative citizens without formal affiliation.
(Large organizations did not participate in this meeting
because it was feared that the articulateness and sophistication of their leaders might inhibit the free expression
of others.)

In addition, there were regular meetings in the neighborhood of the Precinct Community Council, and all who
lived, worked, or had an interest in the community were
urged to attend. Participation was enthusiastic, and it
became apparent that the community was as eager for
change and as willing to help achieve better relations as
we were. It would be an unusual community, we feel, that
would not be equally responsive, once good faith had
been demonstrated by the police. It cannot be said too
often that good law enforcement depends on the reality
of the personal relationship. You cannot have effective
policing without community cooperation, which, in turn,
is impossible in an impersonal atmosphere.

Many policemen fear that the establishment of a citizen
advisory board will somehow result in a diminution of their
authority. Police responsiveness to voiced community
needs, in our view, does not lessen police authority. Moreover, a neighborhood or citizens' advisory committee can
provide the police with an opportunity to present their
point of view to the community. Another salutary by-
product benefits any patrolmen and detectives who attend
the meetings—they learn that mixed among the criticism
and the challenging is a considerable amount of positive
feeling and appreciation of the police effort.

Nevertheless, a limitation on the value of the citizens'
committees has to be recognized: they may represent only
a certain segment of the population. It would be erroneous
to assume automatically that because you have advisory
committees you have good communications and rapport

with the public, and that you are receiving accurate information on the community's perception of the police
operation.

The police must constantly reach out to the people of
the community who are not joiners, who don't appear at
station houses, vocalize complaints, or otherwise maintain contact with the police. Raymond Galvin says of the
Oakland, California, Police Department, "We send out a
bulletin that says we *solicit* complaints. It upsets the
policemen, who say, don't we have enough without you
asking for them? The answer is, no. We have to do more
of it."[4]

As a rule, citizens' advisory committees are less tuned
to grass-roots sentiments than neighborhood advisory
committees. A citizens' committee generally includes
representatives from the clergy, the business community
and possibly the fraternal organizations, some of the leading property owners, and some "police buffs"—people
who just love police and want to be associated with them
in any capacity. The neighborhood committee, on the
other hand, is more apt to be composed of people who
are just living on the block. To reach these people—to say
nothing of those who are far more alienated and hostile—
police must go more than halfway to bring them into some
kind of dialogue.

In the Ninth Precinct we had a community council that
was supposed to be made up of neighborhood people;
however, only middle-class people came to the meetings.
The minority groups—either because they feared they
were not sufficiently articulate to participate or because
they assumed the police would favor the views of the
white middle class—stayed away completely. Finally, we
established another council. The blacks and Puerto Ricans
came to a Mayor's Urban Task Force, and the white mid-

dle class came to a Precinct Community Council—the two forums ensuring that everybody had the opportunity to speak and be heard.

When police restrict themselves to a dialogue with middle-class, so-called titular leaders, they tend to perceive attitudes that are favorable to police; thus they conclude that there are no problems in the neighborhoods. However, since the people who have complaints have not been heard from, such optimistic conclusions are likely to be entirely unwarranted.

A precinct community council exists precisely for the purpose of taking accurate soundings of community sentiment, especially when the community contains several discordant factions. The police should not sit passively in a squat, grey facility and wait to be approached with problems. They must venture into the community to find out what the problems are. Having done this, the police should not shrink from an interpretation of the problems that differ from their own preconceptions. It is necessary to attract as many people as possible into the dialogue. This can be best accomplished by announcing the intention to provide the service that people need and want and by attempting to solve the problems the people want solved.

Police can benefit from community councils in yet another way. Much conflict in urban precincts is due to cross-cultural tensions, and often police are called on to mediate in such flare-ups. As a result, police can find themselves in the uncomfortable position of negotiating between parties whose only forum for the expression of grievances is the station house. Great skill and sensitivity are needed at such times, and in the absence of these qualities, the police will probably absorb much of the anger and hostility that the opposing parties had previously directed against each other. Community councils are extremely good vehicles for supplying disputants a place and a neutral atmosphere for dealing with their mutual problems.

Despite the undoubted value of the programs described, most of the meetings now fail to achieve a very high level of dialogue. Our own need to develop parallel councils is dramatic proof of that. When disputants gather to talk under informal (i.e., undisciplined) circumstances, it is natural to expect a considerable amount of hostile and angry talk, whether between citizen and citizen or citizen and police officer. We all need to learn to experience these meetings on a nonadversative basis, but how is such a thing learned? We would be content if the undesirable behavior produced by angry or hostile feelings could be suppressed. But clearly it would be preferable if basic attitudes producing unproductive behavior could be identified and altered. The question is not: Shouldn't people be more self-disciplined and less angry? This is an irrelevant criticism whenever larger numbers of people, pushed by complex forces that are seldom amenable to the constraints of piety or virtue, are becoming increasingly angry and decreasingly self-disciplined.

The proper question is: How are we going to create a dialogue that can override the incivility, antagonism, and prejudice, and the feelings of anger, fear, and hate?

9. The Human Side

It is taken for granted that a basic, institutional antagonism exists between the police and the various communities with which they have been experiencing difficulties. There seems to be little dispute on this score. In addition, it is more or less assumed that the individuals who take part in the drama of police–community relations at the street level are stuck with the same bad feelings. This is not necessarily true. If the proper setting can be devised, we can eliminate or reduce a certain amount of the stereotyped thinking that is responsible for feelings of fear and anger. "Setting" in this context means a total environmental complex; specifically, it includes a deliberate attempt to deal with the consciousness of *self* of the police officer and of the citizen he confronts.

The process has two aspects. In one, the individual develops an appreciation of what others are actually experiencing. In the second, he increases his own sensitivity with respect to his personal experiences and feelings.

"Operation Empathy" was a dramatic program aimed at heightening the ability of police officers in Covina, California, to use sensitivity in dealing with the citizens. In this project selected officers of the department were booked anonymously into the county jail, to learn what it is like to be imprisoned. One officer who went through the program indicated that the time spent in the cell had changed some of the ideas of many of his fellow participants about the men they arrest. A companion program called "Operation Empathy—Skid Row" has been described by Covina Chief Fred Ferguson:

> Our Covina officers, who were willing to become skid row inhabitants, were carefully selected and conditioned for the role they were about to play. Each man was given three dollars with which to purchase a complete outfit of pawn shop clothing. The only new articles of attire he was allowed was footwear—reject tennis shoes purchased for a few small coins. Among his other props were such items as a shopping bag filled with collected junk, a wine bottle camouflaged with a brown paper sack.
> Conditioned and ready, our men, assigned in pairs, moved into the Los Angeles skid row district. They soon discovered that when they tried to leave the area, walking a few blocks into the legitimate retail

sections, they were told, "Go back where you be-
long!" Our men knew in reality they were not
"bums," but they found that other citizens quickly
characterized them and treated them accordingly.
Some women, when approached on the sidewalk
and asked for a match, stepped out into the street
rather than offer a reply, much less a light for a
smoke.

During the skid row experiment, our men ate in the
rescue missions, and sat through the prayer services with other outcasts and derelicts. They roamed
the streets and alleys, and discovered many level-
ling experiences. Some were anticipated, others
were not.[1]

One presumably unanticipated experience was reported
by a Holyoke, Massachusetts, police officer who went to
Covina to study the project:

One of the officers spent some time on Skid Row in
Los Angeles and was supposed to go as far as getting himself arrested. The officer reported that when
he saw the officers from L.A.P.D. bearing down on
him, he cracked and identified himself. He reported
that he could not believe the feeling that he had
when he thought that he would be arrested.[2]

The "role playing" involved in the California program
is a device that will be familiar to students of sensitivity,
encounter, or t-groups which are formed to enhance self-
insight and improve group dynamics; that is, to acquire
skill in interpersonal relations. It would be hard to name a
skill that would serve a police officer better.

Human interaction groups take as their operating premise that people in a complex, high-speed, increasingly depersonalized society are not encouraged to express their feelings or, indeed, to identify them accurately. It has been well documented that the resultant confusion and inner turmoil are extremely destructive to the tapestry of human relationships constituting the social order.

Groups formed to develop interpersonal dialogue have been utilized in two primary forms in police–community relations work. There are groups composed entirely of police officers and groups composed of policemen interacting with citizens of the community they serve. The first type is exemplified by the "in-house" sensitivity training programs of the Utica, New York, Police Department, sponsored and managed by the department's Community Relations Unit and featuring role-playing activities, interpersonal dialogues, and seminars. In Sausalito, California, the entire force of 27 men holds a monthly sensitivity-training session with a psychologist.

The second type of group is represented by the "panel discussions" held in Indianapolis, Indiana, between police recruits and local teenagers. One observer of these encounters notes that "the kids are open and honest, and the police, from time to time, get terribly up-tight about some of the things the kids have to say." In Buffalo, New York, a similar human-relations training program bringing together police and black community leaders has caused entire classes of police to rise and leave in protest.

In both types of group formation, the individual is expected to speak honestly, openly, and directly—an experience for which the police officer is ill-prepared by his career in a rigid, highly structured and authoritarian system, to say nothing of his daily street experiences.

On the other hand, the New York Police Department's

"Youth Dialogue" program included a mutually successful opportunity for police and precinct youths to evaluate
the problems and frustrations they confront, with particular attention to difficulties that create conflicts between
them. Groups of approximately 30 teenaged boys from
high-hazard areas and ten patrolmen from the same precincts were able to spend weekends together at a camp
in upstate New York. In the relaxed, informal country
atmosphere, the policemen and the youths had a chance
to become acquainted and to develop an understanding
of one another's viewpoints. This rewarding experience
was carried over into daily contacts and furthered by
ongoing programs instituted after the weekend sessions.[3]

Groups of this nature and with these goals have been
utilized (with results that are still difficult to evaluate) in
such diverse communities as Houston, Texas, and Jacksonville, Florida. A police–minority youth encounter group
workshop has been held in Rochester, New York, and
others have taken place at Stanford University and at the
University of Colorado. Since 1968 a Behavioral Interaction Training program has been operating under the joint
auspices of Bellarmine College and the Louisville, Kentucky, Division of Police. Of the experience, Louisville's
Chief C. J. Hyde has said:

> Officers from the rank of Patrolman to Assistant
> Chief of Police have been among the different
> classes completed. The value of this training pro-
> gram in my opinion is best evaluated by the notice-
> able change in attitude in officers of all ranks that
> have completed this two weeks' training toward the
> management problems experienced not only at the
> Chief's Office level but at district and bureau levels.
> Suggestions by the graduates of these classes for
> the betterment of the Department have been more

numerous and when criticism is experienced it is usually accompanied by a suggestion for improvement. The attitudes toward the public served also mirrors the positive aspects to this training program.[4]

Chief Hyde's cautiously optimistic reaction is a view that fairly well reflects our own and that of men like Dr. Melvin P. Sikes, who was the program director of Houston's Cooperative Crime Prevention Program. Dr. Sikes indicated that he had observed visible changes on the part of some of the police officers who participated in the experimental program, but he questioned the permanence of the changes.

The following brief account of one police program displays the mechanics of a human interaction group. The Jacksonville program was sponsored and constructed by the local office of the Anti-Defamation League of B'nai Brith.[5] Insufficient provision was made for identifying the program and its sponsors, and thus some of the eighteen officers going through the 30-hour course were under the mistaken impression that the goal of the course was to create "new policy" for the department. Indeed, one or two refused for a time to be convinced that the ADL was not on the Attorney General's list of subversive organizations.

Despite an inauspicious beginning, the program had several positive aspects—most notably a structural approach that permitted the group itself to retain decision-making powers. This measure proved to be nonthreatening, and it created a relaxed environment. Police officers have been known to resent and resist coercion from "liberal" social scientists, and in this case they were pleasantly surprised when they encountered none. At no point, moreover, were they treated punitively for "incorrect" attitudes or statements. Even officers expressing virulently racist views were not attacked but were led, through patient questioning, to a fuller exposition of their views. Then they were able to consider the possible relationship between their attitudes and the problems they encountered as police officers in dealing with minority members of the community.

At no point was the discussion generalized away from the pragmatic consideration of the police experience. The officers—all sergeants, lieutenants, and captains—held problem-solving discussions of a number of case studies, and this device facilitated an examination of work problems and problems of interpersonal relations. The basic premise of the program was that the police officer is the expert in police work. Consequently, the program coordinators involved the police themselves in the formulations of the sample case studies (and interviewed members of the community to determine how negative contacts with police officers had occurred). Thus the case histories were guaranteed to have relevance and immediacy for the participants.

The policemen first met in the building that housed the Community Relations Division of the Jacksonville Police Department. The consultant, Ronald Cohn of the ADL, surprised the men by appointing one of them to be discussion leader. The spontaneity of group discussion was a new experience for the police officers, and they were not entirely comfortable with it. Some, more familiar with autocratic procedures, would have preferred at least initially to be called on and questioned for their opinions. But they soon adjusted. Given decision-making powers, they first agreed to move into a more intimate, semicircular seating arrangement and then to a room in a different building, where they were able to sit around a table.

Every situation that called for group decisions opened up areas of discussion. For example, they had to decide how people were to be addressed. The ADL man opted for "Ron," but the police officers decided they were more comfortable using last name and rank. This led naturally into a productive exploration of the need for respect and dignified address—not only for themselves but for members of a minority community.

In such a course, understanding can emerge only if the participants, who have been encouraged to probe their deepest feelings, are free to say what they think in an atmosphere of permissiveness, empathy, and group interaction. By and large, participants are allowed to decide what they require in the way of reference data and other source facilities. In the Jacksonville program, a request from the officers for factual information concerning black history led to the showing of the tape of a Xerox television special starring Bill Cosby. This in turn led to a request that members of the black community be brought in for a dialogue. At first the officers agreed that they wanted to meet only "moderate" black leaders. Later they decided they also wanted to meet "militants." The meetings took place during the second week of the program. Many of the police officers had never before talked with black men and women except for impersonal contacts during police activities.

The blacks were relentlessly frank. Three teenaged boys expressed their hatred of police. They enumerated their experiences with the police and their unalterable conviction that police were all head-busters and black police all Toms. The police of course were defensive in response to the charges of police brutality. When the guests had departed and the discussion commenced, however, several remarked candidly that the department had a few people who used excessive force and that abuses of authority did occur. They said that they had seen police who were in fact brutal and that some had earned their reputations by "jumping out and kicking ass." They admitted that they had never seen white men treated the way black men were treated. Some admitted that they personally did not show respect to blacks or the poor.

The questions of respect and self-respect implicit in the disclosures of police abuse of authority surface again and again in the case history discussions. A typical case follows.

Officer Henry and Officer Walter had had a very friendly working relationship. Officer Henry is white, Officer Walter is Negro. Their cordiality cooled, however, and the relationship became quite frigid. Officer Henry was baffled by this. It happened, however, that Officer Walter had some very strong feelings, and a single incident had completely soured him on Henry.

Officer Henry had bought a new pickup, of which he was very proud, and had placed a Confederate emblem on the front bumper. This caused Officer Walter to become very cool toward him. Henry asked what had happened and why Walter was now avoiding him. Deciding to be frank, Officer Walter answered that the reason for his displeasure was the Confederate emblem. Henry was amazed and somewhat angered. He felt that Walter's reaction was completely unjustified, and he said so. Their subsequent discussion went something like this:

HENRY.   What the hell do you mean? What's wrong with having a Confederate flag on my bumper?

WALTER.   That symbol means something special to Negroes. It means support of the slavery days in the South. It's the symbol of resistance against equality. It's used by the Ku Klux Klan and White Citizens' Councils.

HENRY.   I don't care how it's used by some kooks, it shows my loyalty and love for the South. Why shouldn't I show it?

WALTER.   But I find it objectionable. All Negroes find it objectionable. Why should you do anything that's objectionable and so insulting to us?

HENRY.   You mean to say that nobody should be permitted to display that emblem?

WALTER.   I'm not saying that, but you're not just anybody. You're a police officer and you shouldn't express any opinions or seem to be in favor of anything that is prejudiced against any group. As police officers we are in a very special position.

HENRY.   I'll be damned. I think you Negroes are too sensitive. I don't mean any harm and I don't see why I should take that emblem off.

That ended the discussion for the time being at least, and further friendly relations between the two men.

QUESTIONS

1.   What are your reactions to this argument?
2.   Would you have any recommendations in this connection for police officers?

One practical police problem implicit in this case study

—that of black and white officers riding together in the same car—came up the first day and almost every day thereafter. Initially the consensus seemed to be that black and white officers could not ride together because they would have nothing to talk about. Subsequently the group was able to realize that this was not the true reason for the resistance. Though never resolved, the question was discussed in greater depth and with greater honesty each time it arose. This had practical consequences, since the undersheriff of Duval County (Jacksonville) was hoping to establish an integrated patrol system.

Human interaction programs not only serve to correct misconceptions (e.g., stereotyped thinking about race) and to fill in gaps (the Jacksonville officers admitted they knew very little about civil-rights organizations, though holding strong and negative opinions based on what they read in newspapers and heard about from their fellow officers). Such programs also must provide access to human emotions that are normally suppressed by stereo-typed relationships.

During the Jacksonville session, a black policeman broke into the discussion to tell a story about a black soldier serving abroad in the United States Army who was coming home to Georgia. He had written the governor saying how wonderful the state was and that he was returning with his German wife. He then received the following telegram from the governor: "The letter has been lynched; please let us know when you arrive."

All the participants laughed, and then the black officer said, "When you white people tell a joke about black people it generally makes fun of us. When we black peo-ple tell a joke about ourselves, it is about the condition we find ourselves in." This insight marked the first time that the black officer had been able to be honest with the group about his feelings, and he got an honest response from the group in return.

At the conclusion of the two-week project some of the white officers said they thought that the course had been valuable. Since it was an isolated experience, however, none felt that it would have any significant effect on their attitudes, nor that it would have any meaningful impact on police performance in Jacksonville. They expressed the hope that the course would be part of a larger program of training, and they looked forward to an effective follow-up program.[6]

A similar program undertaken by Edward S. Rosenbluh and William A. Reichart at Bellarmine College, Louisville, Kentucky, recognized the distaste felt by many policemen for the term "police–community relations" and labeled itself a "Police Leadership Seminar." Like the Jacksonville project, the Louisville seminar stressed on-the-job problem solving. The program directors went a step further in establishing the premise of the program by accompanying the officers during their duty hours (day and night) to observe their problems and procedures. Thus, the project developed respect in the eyes of many of the participants for the role of ombudsman:

> A particularly significant result was the feeling evinced by most participants that someone was concerned about their needs and feelings and would perhaps be in a position to communicate to the top command their frustrations and suggestions anonymously.[7]

The authors describe their work as the "Small Group Interaction Approach." Present with twelve to fifteen officers were two program directors, who sat opposite each other. While one spoke, the other monitored the group for lack of interest or failure of comprehension. This meant that there was considerable professional supervision, which the Jacksonville project had dispensed with.

Reflecting later on the sensitivity aspects of the program, the project sponsors felt that the loss in professional control was more than balanced by the honesty invoked by having "one of their own" lead the discussions. In any case, they asserted their belief that unstructured sensitivity work is inherently less effective (and potentially more dangerous) than the job-related encounter focusing on work problems. In this we heartily concur. We are hopeful that changes in perception will result in altered field behavior even if the new insights are not supported by actual changes in attitude, which are extremely difficult to achieve. Thus the community can benefit from the sensitivity training of a brutal or prejudiced officer who comes to see that he can best perform his duties if he alters his manner of handling police problems. He may still refuse to be moved in his fundamental attitudes, but a change for the better has occurred.

We also agree wholeheartedly that police officers should not have to confront hostile people until they have indicated that they are ready to. No matter how carefully an encounter program is controlled, the expression of hostility will leave a residue of bad feeling unless both parties are prepared to "risk all" and expose themselves fully to each other. At present, few blacks and police officers are able to achieve such candor in sessions together.

We do not discount the value of benefits that can accrue from honest interaction. There is some relief from pent-up feelings and (particularly on the part of minority citizens) from a sense of anxiety and isolation. One of the more encouraging findings of the Rochester, New York, police–minority youth workshop was that the young black men who participated became somewhat more confident that they could affect interactions with police. This attitude was "opposed to feeling that the environment was in complete control of their destiny. . . . This would seem an important finding inasmuch as feeling that one is at the mercy of one's environment almost exclusively is a powerfully debilitating experience for most human beings."[8]

Significantly, policemen are not exempt from the feeling just described. The reports on the Jacksonville experience note that the police officers manifested "inferiority feelings" and were uncomfortable with the knowledge that they were going to control the meetings. In a hierarchy authority comes with increasing rank, but for many police officers there is no corresponding increase in inner authority. There is consequent dependence on external forms—an authoritarian discipline–punishment syndrome —and reluctance to risk the far more difficult task of maintaining authority by voluntarily expressing human feelings and engaging in interaction with other people. Whereas some maintain authority through the threat of punishment, using the distance–alienation–law-enforcement–obedience approach, it is more desirable to accomplish the same goal by calling on cooperation, friendship, identity, empathy, and service. The same type of interaction that passes between police administrators and middle-rank managers and between middle-rank managers and patrolmen also passes between the police and their "enemies" in the citizen population.

Under the heading of "authoritarianism," Allport has the following:

> Living in a democracy is a higgledy-piggledy affair. Finding it so, prejudiced people sometimes declare that America should not be a democracy, but merely

a "republic."' The consequences of personal freedom they find unpredictable. Individuality makes for
indefiniteness, disorderliness, and change.
To avoid such slipperiness the prejudiced person
looks for hierarchy in society. Power arrangements
are definite—something he can understand and
count on. He likes authority, and says that what
America needs is "more discipline." By discipline,
of course, he means *outer* discipline, preferring, so
to speak, to see people's backbones on the outside
rather than on the inside. . . .
This need for authority reflects a deep distrust of
human beings. Earlier . . . we noted the tendency of
prejudiced people to agree that "the world is a
hazardous place where men are basically evil and
dangerous." Now, the essential philosophy of democracy is the reverse. It tells us to trust a person
until he proves himself untrustworthy. The prejudiced person does the opposite. He distrusts every
person untli he proves himself trustworthy.[9]

To maintain between police and community the undemocratic relationship described by Allport is to legitimize in
the society, retrospectively, a pattern of child rearing that
tends to produce undesirable characteristics, including
prejudice:

Mothers of prejudiced children, *far more often*
than the mothers of unprejudiced children, held
that:

Obedience is the most important thing a child can
learn.

A child should never be permitted to set his will
against that of his parents.

A child should never keep a secret from his
parents.

I prefer a quiet child to one who is noisy.

(In the case of temper tantrums) Teach the child

that two can play that game, by getting angry yourself.

In the case of sex play (masturbation) the mother of
the prejudiced child is much more likely to believe
she should punish the child. . . .

What does such a style of child training do to a
child? For one thing it puts him on guard. He has
to watch his impulses carefully. Not only is he pun-
ished for them when they counter the parents' con-
venience and rules, as they frequently do, but he
feels at such times that love is withdrawn from him.
When love is withdrawn he is alone, exposed, deso-
late. Thus he comes to watch alertly for signs of
parental approval or disapproval. It is they who have
power, and they who give or withhold their condi-
tional love. Their power and their will are the deci-
sive agents in the child's life.
What is the result? First of all, the child learns that
power and authority dominate human relationships
—not trust and tolerance. The stage is thus set for
a hierarchical view of society. Equality does not
really prevail. The effect goes deeper. The child
mistrusts his impulses: he must not have temper
tantrums, he must not disobey, he must not play
with his sex organs. He must fight such evil in himself. Through a simple act of projection . . . the
child come to fear evil impulses in others. They
have dark designs; their impulses threaten the child;
they are not to be trusted.[10]

Human relations seminars will not find it desirable to
probe too deeply the parallels between the emotions of
the child and the emotion of a typical patrolman on duty.
Inevitably, however, the police officer will be the gainer as
he becomes more familiar with the reasons for his own
feelings and attitudes and learns how they help to determine what happens to him as he performs his duties.

A properly organized human-relations training program should help uncover these submerged relationships. Thus the police and civilian participants can come to recognize that many of the unsatisfactory aspects of their previous interrelations were not intrinsic to police–citizen contact but were imposed on them by the rigid structure that identifies the officer as a law enforcer and the citizen as a potential law breaker.

Human interaction seminars—when considered as nothing more than another item in a portfolio of investments of time and energy and enthusiasm and hope—are scarcely the manna from heaven that many proponents claim. Yet they have more significance than is suggested by their shortcomings. Increased self-insight is an important method for helping to create the consciousness that "we" and "they" are actually "us." And that, ultimately, is the goal of police–community relations. We must begin to operate so that the police are part of and not apart from the community they serve. And that cannot happen unless the individuals who enact the drama of "community" know what they are talking about.

10. Crisis Intervention

Analysis of the typical patrolman's duty hours suggests that crime control and law enforcement account for only slightly more than 10 percent of his time. The balance involves the maintenance of order, the providing of services, or simply the gathering of information. Included in such activities are all those police areas in which the patrolman—the lowest in the police hierarchy—exercises the greatest autonomy and personal discretion. Many duties involve citizens in conflict with each other for whom the police intervention may or may not be desirable and may or may not be desired. In *Varieties of Police Behavior*, James Q. Wilson writes that the difficult task of maintaining order "is further exacerbated by the fact that the patrolman's discretion is exercised in an emotional, apprehensive, and perhaps hostile environment."[1]

In this area the law is least well defined, the patrolman's discretionary powers are the greatest, and police duties entail the greatest risk of harm. The New York Police Department, for example, estimates that 40 percent of injuries are incurred responding to calls of family disturbances. A report of the Federal Bureau of Investigation notes that 22 percent of policemen killed in the line of duty died while responding to complaints of "disturbances," and prominent among these disruptions of the public order are calls concerning "family fights."[2] One experienced public official puts these events second in frequency only to motor-vehicle accidents. Consequently, we have this distressing circumstance: the individual officer responding to a recurring and hazardous type of call has virtually total discretion; yet typically he has received no special training for the duty.

Wilson describes the dilemma of the policeman called on to resolve a family dispute:

> A typical case, one which I witnessed many times, involves a wife with a black eye telling the patrolman she wants her husband who she alleges hit her, "thrown out of the house." The officer knows he has no authority to throw husbands out of their homes and he tells her so. She is dissatisfied. He suggests she file a complaint, but she does not want her husband arrested. She may promise to make a complaint the next morning, but the patrolman knows

from experience that she will probably change her mind later. If the officer does nothing about the quarrel he is "uncooperative"; if he steps in he is in the danger of exceeding his authority. Some patrolmen develop ways of mollifying everyone, others get out as quickly as they can, but all dislike such situations and find them awkward and risky.[3]

The foregoing, of course, has said nothing of the cost to the public order from "family fight" incidents. In 1971 in New York City there were 1466 homicides. Of these, 50 percent involved transactions between people who were either related or known to each other.[4] Thus family disputes should provide a fruitful area for police–community relations techniques designed to strengthen the police's order-maintaining function and simultaneously to brighten the police image. If people are to view the police as an integral and beneficial component of the community structure, the police must improve the social service aspects of their mission.

With calls for family crisis intervention, for example, police should begin to recognize that the traditional authoritarian approach is repugnant to most people. This is the method that has been utilized traditionally, and it has not been as successful as its proponents claim. As often as not, the intervening policeman experiences hostility (and frequently assaults) that he unwittingly has called down on himself. A dramatic incident was described in the *New York Tmes Magazine*:

From inside the man roars "You come in and I'll blow your ———— head off." With that a burly sergeant pushes by the woman and bangs on the door. "Let's go! Open up or we'll kick it down," he shouts. "Come right ahead ————" the man bellows back.[5]

It was later discovered that the apartment-dweller had attempted to fire his gun at the sergeant through the door and that only a faulty firing pin had saved the officer from harm. The incident reveals—and statistics repeatedly verify—that a blustery show of personal authority not only does not work but frequently endangers the officer in a way that might have been averted by another approach.

If police behavior in family crisis intervention is to change, the police must relearn the function of the intervention and must acquire a heightened awareness of the dynamics of human interaction. Furthermore, these altered patterns of behavior must be reinforced until they can influence strongly held attitudes and biases. A pilot program attempting to achieve all these goals commenced in New York City's 30th Precinct in May 1967. An evaluation of the program offers persuasive data: During the two years that the newly created Family Crisis Intervention Unit was being studied, its members intervened on 1388 calls, involving 962 families, in a patrol area of 85,000 population.[6] The members of the special unit incurred no injuries, and the community responded positively to the unit. Moreover, what Henry S. Ruth, Jr., then director of the National Institute of Law Enforcement and Criminal Justice, calls "the basic professional identity" of the unit's officers remained undisturbed.

Two Ph.D.'s—former New York City policemen Morton Bard, the project director, and Bernard Berkowitz, the project supervisor—wanted to demonstrate that innovative techniques could achieve traditional goals with a minimal departure from usual police practice and performance. The training program, they recognized, would have to develop skills that the participating police officers could sustain only with "significant alteration of the interpersonal perceptual set."[7] The eighteen officers selected for the program (comprising about 10 percent of the force

of the 30th Precinct on the Upper West Side of Manhattan)
went through a training program designed primarily to
encourage *"gradual change over time* in personal attitudes and values in order to develop necessary interpersonal objectivity"[8] (italics ours).

The projects had three phases. In the preparatory phase
the officers were selected and trained. In the operational
phase the officers functioned within the precinct as the
Family Crisis Intervention Unit (FCIU). And in the final
phase the data accumulated during the operational phase
were analyzed and evaluated (and compared with data
from control Precinct 24, just to the south) in terms of the
following crime control criteria:

1. Total number of family disturbance complaints.
2. Recurrence of complaints by the same families.
3. Total number of homicides.
4. Total number of homicides within the family structure.
5. Total number of assaults.
6. Total number of assaults within the family structure.
7. Total injuries sustained by intervening patrolmen.

The patrolmen selected (all volunteers) had between
three and ten years of service. Nine were black, nine
white. The four-week, full-time training program commenced with introduction to and familiarization with the
concept that psychological factors underlie observable
behavior. Morning lectures were followed by afternoon
workshops and small group discussions for which the participants were divided into three groups of six. Each group
was led by a person trained in group psychotherapy.
According to one group leader:

> These (policemen) were all men raised and edu-
> cated in an ethic in which behavior is viewed as

either good or bad and is to be responded to accordingly. I saw my first objective as training the
men to see behavior as being purposive, having a
cause or motivation and comprehensible objective.
I attempted to teach the men that emotions have a
language of their own where neither right or wrong
or even logic prevails.[9]

During the second week the training emphasized "the
family." The officers were encouraged to develop an
understanding of their own feelings, particularly with
respect to such "difficult" areas as sexuality, money,
parent–child conflicts, alcoholism, and feelings of fear
and depression. The ongoing self-exploration addressed
itself to a hidden factor in police procedures: how and
how much these feelings affect performance. During a
later phase of the work, this mechanism was dramatized
for one officer, who in Bard and Berkowitz's description

found that he "turned off" and let his partner take
over whenever they had to deal with a man who had
been drinking. Even if the man was not drunk he
couldn't interest himself in trying to communicate
or relate except in the most perfunctory ways. The
effect was one of indifference or contempt so that
the partner's task was made more difficult. During
one of the sessions the other members of the group
observed that the officer in question always took the
side of the woman in such instances. As he talked
about his feelings of irritation with men who had
drinking problems he connected his reaction to a
family experience with alcoholism. The experience
was not pursued in depth but it served to illustrate
how his personal prejudice had interfered with
effectiveness in family crisis intervention. While he
had subscribed to the principle of "impartiality" he
could not have attained the ability to refrain from
taking sides without such group sessions.[10]

At the end of the second week the officers were paired, on the basis of completed sociograms, into nine biracial teams. Each two-man team was to ride in the FCIU radio car and answer family disturbance calls anywhere within the precinct. Thus the third week of training emphasized conflict resolution and intervention techniques. A supplement to the lectures and small group sessions introduced during this week was similar in many respects to role-playing and psychodrama activities. The Family Crisis Laboratory Demonstrations consisted of short family disturbance dramas played by professional actors who had been instructed to adjust their behavior to conform reactively to the behavior of the team of intervening officers. Each drama was repeated three times (for the benefit of the remaining twelve officers in the audience), and the variations allowed each officer to identify and evaluate his own role in producing the positive or negative outcome of his intervention in a family crisis. Thus the participants not only learned specific behaviors but, equally important, they were gradually led to subtly modify and adjust their personal values and attitudes and to heighten their self-understanding.

Group discussions continued during the final week, but the morning lectures were replaced by field trips to various health and welfare agencies, in the hope of exemplifying the concept of social service. However, the officers learned that social help agencies, along with most other government bureaucracies, are frustrating to deal with, inadequate to meet the challenge facing them, and wasteful of money and effort.

On July 1, 1967, the FCIU radio car was assigned to a sector of the 30th Precinct. When not specifically involved in family intervention, the unit provided normal patrol services. Thus the officers' identity was not compromised, nor were they subjected to the alienation, rejection, and scorn which are often accorded the specialist among generalists. Typically, as Bard and others have noted, the policeman is inclined to view the youth patrolman or the community relations officer as somehow less a policeman.

Since the FCIU officers were performing all the normal police functions in addition to their family crisis intervention specialty, however, they were not ostracized. On the contrary, the effectiveness of their work during the ensuing 22 months encouraged other officers of the precinct to ask them for advice.

One of the officers, 32-year-old Patrolman John E. Bodkin, was a cigar-smoking, seven-year veteran of the force. Bodkin describes how he handled a difficult intervention:

> It was up on 145th Street. And the couple was from the South. We went in there and I could see right off that this guy was tight, very tight. He was a Negro fellow, about 21 or 22 years old, only up in New York six months. She had called the police because of a dispute—a minor thing. But there he was, a little guy, and he was really tense because when we walked in with our uniforms and sticks, you could see that his earlier associations with police officers must have been very rough.
>
> You could see the fear in his eyes, the hostility in his face. His fists were clenched and he was ready to do combat with us. God knows what he would have done if he'd had a gun or a knife. I moved toward the kitchen table and opened my blouse and told him in a nice quiet way that I wanted to talk to him, but he's still looking at my stick. Well, the stick is under my arm so I hung it up on a nearby chair purposely, to show there's no intent here. "Look, I don't need it," I'm trying to say to this guy. "I don't need to because you're a nice guy in my eyes. You don't threaten me, so I'm not going to threaten you."

I've got to show this guy that I'm not a bully, a brute, a Nazi or the Fascist he thinks all cops are.

So he calms down a little. Then I took my hat off and said, "Do you mind if I smoke?" And he looks funny at me. And I say "I'm a cigar smoker and some people don't like the smell of a cigar in their house, so would you mind if I smoke?" And the guy says, "Oh sure, sure," and you could see he was shocked. I felt he saw a human side of us, that I had respect for him and his household.

Then the guy sat down and he and his wife proceed to tell us what it was all about. When we explain to her why he's upset she smiles. "Yes, yes, yes!" You see, she thinks we're on her side. Then we tell him why he's mad and he smiles. "Yes, yes, yes." Now we're on his side. Well, they eventually shake our hands; they were happy and we never had another call from them.[11]

Thus we see that family crisis intervention training has given the officer the skill and insight to approach a difficult and previously frustrating police task and to perform a limited but concrete service. "The provocative hostile behavior of others has been redefined for what it is, helpless and inadequate. The capacity to resist being reduced to this level has been defined as strength."[12] That this redefinition needs considerable encouragement is underlined in the New York City Police Department's Guidelines for Demonstrations, which tells the officer "Your courage and manhood is proved by keeping cool." It further notes that "your real strength" is verified "by your self-restraint."[13] In this connection, Berkowitz has written:

With the police, we have suggested that self-esteem is not necessarily diminished if the patrolman refrains from aggression in the face of insulting or disrespectful behavior. Instead, it has been pro-

posed that violent response to provocation implies
some deficiency of self-regard. It has been necessary to deal with the "masculine mystique" which
has helped make police so malleable in the hands
of those who are determined to provoke violence.
. . . In the course of our project these considerations
of self-esteem have become incorporated into the
value system of the officers and supported by group
pressures and sanctions. The skillful and effective
officer is recognized as one who can defuse a situation to the point where the participants are no
longer in unreasonable rage and can start talking
sense to each other.[14]

Berkowitz suggests that adapting the methods of his
project for use in training police recruits could have important benefits, notably to help encourage a view of the
police "as benign and helpful authorities instead of the
too prevalent view of them as wholly repressive and unal-
terably insensitive."[15] The effect of such a change on
police–community relations can hardly be overempha-
sized. Like other projects that encourage and reward the
officer for referring to his strong and perhaps submerged
motivation for service, rather than his strong and less
well-submerged instinct for control, this project was favorably received by the community. Unit members reported an
increase in the number of referrals originating in families
previously served, and there was also an increase in the
number of families showing up at the station house in
search of an FCIU member. During patrol tours in the unit
car, officers noted a significant decrease in citizen tension
and an equally significant increase in community recognition of the "special cops." The community welcomed
the unit as an improvement of police service. Most telling
were the statistics: during the entire project, the unit sustained no injuries in the course of almost 1400 interven-

tions. During the same time, however, two members of the regular patrol of the precinct (and at least one in the control precinct) did sustain injuries.[16]

In an attempt to replicate the successful Bard–Berkowitz project, investigators at the University of Louisville developed a comparable project that included such modifications as videotape instant replay of the simulated crisis intervention dramas. All recruits in the New York Police Department now receive family crisis intervention training, as do recruits in many other departments.

11. Storefronts

Like other bureaucracies, police departments are saddled with many ills that are related to the bureaucratic structure. Of these, the depersonalization of contact induces the greatest dysfunction insofar as police and community are concerned. For many people, the police station is a grim, fear-provoking (and unlikely) place to go for aid and assistance. Yet at the same time, and for the same people, it is their primary source of aid and assistance. Whereas a middle-class family might consult a psychotherapist over a serious domestic problem, a lower-middle-class family is more likely to present a similar case to the patrolman who answers the disturbance call. Often, problems of welfare, social and health services, medical assistance, and the like come to the attention of the police before the appropriate social agency learns of their existence.

Therefore, any device that increases the willingness of the citizen to see the police as part of the network of community resource agencies is extremely desirable. New York's receptionist program has that value. The same department's storefront center experiments go even further, by making the police more accessible, and by operating in an environment that will be more reassuring to the average citizen.

The storefront center is an effort to decentralize the police presence, making the police more responsive to the local situation by allowing for an increase in citizen input and moving the police out of the central facility and further into the community.

The primary objection to storefront centers has been the tendency to make them into public relations operations. However, the success of the storefront will be proportional to the amount of resistance to this pressure.

Of course there is nothing wrong with public relations efforts that help to increase the public's understanding of police effort and its sympathy for police problems, but they should remain incidental activities. The main function of the facility is the improvement of police service and, to the extent possible, all municipal service.

Well-run storefronts usually have a well-developed information-imparting and referral role. The initial problems for a commander of such a facility involve familiarizing people with its presence and persuading them that its main function is, indeed, service.

The author (L.S.) had a storefront on 125th Street, manned by uniformed police officers, mostly during the hours between noon and 9:00 P.M. In all candor, it has to be recorded that this facility was organized primarily as a public relations device. But we soon discovered that we could provide unique services. We had frequent visits from people of the Harlem community who had problems that we could not handle but were able to refer to other city agencies. Subsequently, we developed informational programs for groups of students or adults. We opened our doors to such neighborhood groups as block associations for meetings. There were standing police exhibits, primarily from the Emergency Service division, and guest speakers from the detective division came to address the community on problems of robbery and burglary, assaults, and swindles. From time to time a trailer containing a narcotics exhibit was parked near the storefront to provide information and literature on narcotics abuse. Inside the storefront we stocked literature on safety, job opportunities, educational opportunities, and the like.

On the Lower East Side, the author (J.F.) instituted an unofficial storefront. We commenced operations with an indoctrination of the uniformed personnel who were going to man the storefront. The speaker, a professional from a neighborhood social agency, not only discussed the social service philosophy but also gave an overview of the city resources available and the services they could provide. The facility quickly became a focal point in the neighborhood. Almost immediately young and old ventured in or peered in to see what the police were doing. Soon we received visits from people with information on gambling and narcotics activity. They were anxious to pass their knowledge on to the police, but they indicated that they were afraid to go to the police station for fear of being labeled as informers. On another front, I recall particularly the woman who brought her two children in, announced that she was going to commit suicide, and requested the officer to please see that her mother got the kids.

As these brief descriptions suggest, the storefront operations fulfilled valuable functions. We realized, however, that the storefronts answered a deeper need in the community for police presence and identification. Both these qualities were diminished considerably when the radio car supplanted the patrolman on the post. The storefront is almost like the return of the foot patrolman. In fact, the Lower East Side program overcame some objections within the department (from those who viewed storefronts as a fragmentation of police power and a drain on manpower for patrol and other services) by having the officer stand out on the street unless he was required for services inside. He became, in essence, a foot patrolman, but a sophisticated one, since he offered extra resources for community service.

There can be no doubt of the desire of people to identify the police as "their own." A management survey of New York's police facilities, noting the growing expense of maintaining and manning numerous separate precinct houses, and given the improvement in communications since many of the houses were built, recommended that a number of buildings be closed and the precincts be combined. As soon as this intent became known, a tremendous hue and cry arose in the communities, which strongly desired to maintain local police representation at least at the level that existed.

In our view, the pressing need is not for increased centralization of service facilities. On the contrary. A logical extension of the storefront principle would be decentralization into storefront headquarters serving not

only the aforementioned purposes but having the autonomy and organizational flexibility to deal with many kinds
of local problems. Such an innovation would go a long
way toward answering the public's need for a community-
oriented police.

In any case, the storefront needs to be manned by wel-
trained officers for whom the concept of service is not
burdensome. In retrospect, we are not satisfied either
with the training or the manner of selection of the officers
who manned the storefronts. There was insufficient training, and the officers were chosen and assigned to duty
in a haphazard manner.

Later storefronts developed a more sophisticated concept of their role in the community, implicitly based on
the presumption that all policemen are "community-rela-
tions" officers. The storefront center maintained by the
author (J.F.) on the Lower East Side of Manhattan was
to have been jointly manned by police officers and social
workers. The police were to be involved in an educational
program at a graduate school of social work, for which
they would get college credits. They were volunteers,
selected on the basis of general ability, special skills,
language facility, race, and ethnic origins, as well as a
predisposition toward the broadest view of the nature
of police work.

A storefront of this sort points toward a community-
oriented police that, having received from police superiors
a general definition of the police problem in its area of
responsibility, then refines the definition, together with the
local community and on its own initiative. Such a unit implies the existence of a considerable amount of personal
authority and accountability at the lower ranges of the
police hierarchy, as well as ready civilian access to decision-making at a level of policy that bears on their lives.

Contrary to what some might think, such plans for decentralization are favorably received by a number of police administrators. Good storefront programs exist in Dayton, Ohio, Holyoke, Massachusetts, St. Louis, Missouri, Los Angeles, California, and Louisville, Kentucky. These are experimental programs, and preliminary data are promising. As things stand now, the major stumbling block to increased decentralization, increased responsibility and accountability for the patrolman, and increased responsiveness to community input is the debased position of the police in the eyes of the public.

12. Minority Recruitment

Being a policeman in New York City is a pretty good job for the typical high school graduate. He can earn $15,000 a year, get a five-week vacation, have unlimited sick leave, and look forward to retirement in 20 years at half pay. There are, of course, negative aspects as well—hazards and pressures not found on an ordinary job. All things considered, however, a drive to recruit young black men, who are acknowledged to be disproportionately represented among the unemployed and underemployed population, should have some success. Yet a number of cities have initiated such drives, with few positive results.

Figures for key cities indicate the extent of the disparity between the black population and the proportion of black officers on police forces.[1]

Cities	% Black	Total Police Force	Total Black Police	% Black Police
Washington, D.C.	71.1	4,994	1,797	35.9
Newark, N.J.	54.2	1,500	225	15.0
Gary, Ind.	52.8	415	130	31.0
Atlanta, Ga.	51.3	942	260	28.0
Baltimore, Md.	46.4	3,300	420	13.0
New Orleans, La.	45.0	1,359	83	6.1
Detroit, Mich.	43.7	5,100	567	12.0
Wilmington, Del.	43.6	277	32	11.5
Birmingham, Ala.	42.0	660	13	1.9
St. Louis, Mo.	40.9	2,221	326	14.0
Portsmouth, Va.	39.9	195	14	7.5
Jackson, Miss.	39.3	270	17	6.2
Memphis, Tenn.	38.9	1,090	55	5.0
Cleveland, Ohio	38.3	2,445	191	7.7
Mobile, Ala.	35.5	277	36	13.3
Oakland, Calif.	34.5	713	34	4.7
Winston-Salem, N.C.	34.3	300	20	6.6
Shreveport, La.	33.9	345	25	7.2
Philadelphia, Pa.	33.6	7,242	1,347	18.6
Chicago, Ill.	32.6	12,678	2,100	16.5
Dayton, Ohio	30.5	422	22	4.1
Hartford, Conn.	27.9	500	60	12.0
Pittsburgh, Pa.	20.2	1,640	105	6.4
Dallas, Tex.	24.9	1,640	32	1.9
Miami, Fla.	22.7	719	74	10.0
New York, N.Y.	21.2	31,700	2,400	7.5
Los Angeles, Calif.	17.9	6,705	350	5.2
Boston, Mass.	16.3	2,807	60	2.1
Milwaukee, Wis.	14.7	2,098	50	2.3
San Francisco, Calif.	13.4	1,800	90	5.0

Both the President's Commission on Law Enforcement and Administration of Justice and the National Advisory Commission on Civil Disorders deemed it imperative, particularly in urban areas, that law enforcement agencies become more representative of minority communities. Increased recruitment of minorities, integration of personnel use, and equal opportunity for promotion to all ranks were seen to be critical prerequisites for achieving a more harmonious relationship between the police and minority communities. Many police organizations instituted stepped-up recruitment programs, including cadet programs and projects in special training and in preparation for exams. At best, these efforts have obtained the most limited success.

To show the dimensions of the problem, let us take a not atypical case. There are approximately 900 state troopers in Massachusetts. Of these, one is black. Having set itself the modest goal of ten additional black troopers (a total of 1 percent of the force in a state in which blacks comprise about 3 percent of the population) the state Department of Public Safety launched a drive to recruit blacks. Statewide, a total of 100 young men responded. Of these applicants, only two were appointed, and one of the two was subsequently dropped for failure to satisfy a requirement to swim 50 yards.

If underrepresentation of minorities on police forces continues as at present, the best efforts to solve the problems that have appeared within the system and within the guidelines established by police organizations for recruitment will have proved to be inadequate. Our guess is such pessimism is justified. Why is the police image in minority communities such a severe bar to recruitment that the executive director of the Massachusetts Urban Coalition believes that his own credibility would be damaged if he became actively involved in the recruitment of young blacks for police work?

The extent of the resistance may be inferred by the statistics for the New York City department. For the last 20 years, New York's complement of black officers has been about 5 to 6 percent. To increase the number of black officers, the city engaged in a concentrated drive that included saturation recruitment in black neighborhoods by teams of black and white officers working street corners with a radio car, a billboard, and application forms, as well as mail reminders that an examination was forthcoming. Despite all this, the percentage of black officers on the force rose only to 7.5 percent (2,400 out of 31,700). The stereotype of the police officers as a repressive and abusive maintainer of the status quo proves again and again to be stronger than potential economic and social gains in motivating the individual applicant.

The ultimate solution to the problem does not lie within the recruitment program, but within the police operation itself. To the extent that the police operation justifies itself to the minority community, relations will improve, and an increasing number of young black men, with a minimum of encouragement, will find police work a suitable career. In the meantime, however, it is essential that police recruiting efforts address factors that produce the resistance. The negative police image is a compound of the following elements:

1. The black community has generally experienced white policemen as being hostile and abusive. Consequently, it has been extremely difficult for the typical black person (unlike the typical white person) to see the police force as a service profession operating in the community interest.

2. Blacks have had a significant number of negative experiences with black policemen who have internalized the less humane aspects of the law enforcement system and who, as a result, are not the models the black community would choose for its youth to emulate. These two factors conspire to encourage the belief that change cannot be made by joining the establishment, that becoming part of the system will require the young black to engage in acts of repression against his brothers and sisters.

Even if neither of the foregoing statements were true, few blacks would be attracted to a system that gives internal signs of discrimination. Out of frustration, those blacks already in the department transmit negative feelings about their work assignments and opportunities for promotion. In many cases, there is totally inadequate diffusion of black personnel throughout the department (e.g., into such prestige jobs as detective). At present any potential applicant bright enough to qualify probably experiences considerable anxiety about what it would be like to work in a largely white police force. Even the recent mild increases in black representation on police forces have produced unmistakable signs of increasing tensions between black and white policemen. Black policemen seen to mirror the feelings of the black community toward white police officers and toward the force itself, and this input is one of the primary benefits derived from their presence. They have tended to believe that duty assignments and appointive promotional opportunities are inequitable; that white officers lack community awareness and concern; that white officers do not enforce the law; that when white officers do enforce the law they are unnecessarily aggressive, resort to force prematurely, and are reflexively abusive in manner; that white officers display contempt for blacks through verbal abuse and discourtesy; that white officers engage in corrupt practices that victimize blacks; that white officers harass black officers by not recognizing them and by questioning their police credentials in off-duty situations; that superior officers fail to exercise the necessary controls over conduct and attitudes of white officers.

The Guardians of Michigan, an organization of black law enforcement officials, has not assumed the posture of some of the more radical black police organizations, yet it has become increasingly vocal about the growing frustration and alienation of black officers. The January 1971 newsletter of the Guardians said:

> It is common knowledge among veteran black police officers that the climate at most police precincts is not conducive to the occupational growth of young uniformed black patrolmen or black uniformed supervisory officers below the rank of inspector. . . . One of the basic tenets of the racist theory is the black man is inferior to the white man, and is not to be trusted with the power or the trapping of power which the uniformed military and police official represents. Consequently, the greatest threat to an institution built on a foundation of racism is a large influx of black uniformed police officers at all levels. Such an increase would undoubtedly cause unusual reactions. The racist value system would have to undergo change and a new system structured, sensitive to the needs of the majority of Detroit citizens.

Other all-black police organizations, like the Officers for Justice and the National Society of Afro-American

Policemen, identify themselves *primarily* with the black community. San Francisco's Officers for Justice has exemplified the new militancy with this statement:

> We will no longer permit ourselves to be relegated to the role of brutal pawns in a chess game, affecting the communities in which we serve. We are husbands, fathers, brothers, neighbors and members of the black community. Donning the blue uniform has not changed this. On the contrary, it has sharpened our perception of our responsibilities as black males in a society seemingly unresponsive to the needs of black people. We see our role as the role of a protector of this community, and this is the role we intend to fulfill.

In the face of this excoriating rhetoric, what are departments doing to lower the black community's resistance to police work? Basically, nothing. Some people in the police establishment do not want more blacks in the police, and they resist a black presence because of various beliefs, including the following: that standards are being lowered to admit minorities; that lowered standards impair the concept of professionalization; that there exists a double standard of internal discipline favoring black officers; that preference is given to blacks in duty assignments and appointive promotional positions; that black officers are not loyal to the police department or to the code that officer supports brother officer; that black officers interfere with white officers attempting to arrest violators of the law; that black officers ignore abuse of and even assaults on white officers by minorities; that black officers are sympathetic to militant groups like the Panthers; that black officers identify with antilaw groups in speech and in appearance; that political interference favors blacks and hampers white officers in the performance of their sworn duty.

Underlying all the foregoing complaints is the psychological fact that increased numbers of blacks are perceived to threaten the occupational image of many white police officers. Studies in Crime and Law Enforcement in Major Metropolitan Areas, undertaken for the President's Commission on Law Enforcement, found that four out of five white policemen working in predominantly black neighborhoods in Chicago, Washington, and Boston were "highly prejudiced and extremely anti-Negro" or "prejudiced and anti-Negro." (Three out of ten black policemen also fell into these two categories.) Given such attitudes, efforts at increased recruitment suffer not only from lack of imagination, which could be overcome with a bit of effort, but from faulty implementation and sabotage of efforts that are made.

To overcome these difficulties, new approaches are needed, and if the solutions involve measures that do not conform to the present system, the system will have to be altered to conform to the solutions. This process will in turn create new problems, as there would be, for example, if a force were to commit itself to so-called lowering of standards for the purpose of increasing minority representation. Some internal resistance can be met by educational methods, but some is likely to be residual and will have to be endured.

The first step toward increasing minority representation on police departments is the creation in each city of a task force composed of all interested elements in the community, including police administration, representatives of police unions, civic leaders, spokesmen with standing and credibility in the minority community, and young people. The broader the base of representation, the better. The group must have policy-making powers in all areas that now contain significant bars to minority recruitment, such as those just named, examination procedures, standards, and occupational equality of opportunity. The task force must exist for the sole purpose of correcting an imbalance in the ethnic and social makeup of the police force; and its goal must be subscribed to by the city's top police administrator.

The group must be authorized to recruit, hire, and train police personnel and to devise entrance standards for the force that accord with the realities of police work today. Contrary to the belief of some, this does not mean the lowering of standards, but it does imply that better systems must be devised for integrating young black men into an organization that has heretofore responded with fear and suspicion to indications of black pride and identity. Statistics bear out repeatedly that the greatest tensions, the greatest hostility, and the most distressing contacts between police and blacks occur precisely with that portion of the black population which is young and male. The task force must recruit for a police force that welcomes members whose consciousness and loyalty are primarily invested in the black community. This sentiment has been expressed by Patrolman Renault Robinson, executive director of the Afro-American Patrolman's League in Chicago: "What the black policeman is beginning to get away from is that old thing of being a Tom. Before, we've always been the good mercenary in a colonial situation. Now we're saying we're black men first and policemen second." [2]

In other words, the task force for recruiting must make it known that *the black applicant is being sought in order to change the system*. To back up such a claim, a task force will need to support its rhetoric by its actions. It will probably have recruitment teams and mobile units. How are the men selected? What is known of each team member's personal commitment to the goal of increased minority representation in the police organization? The care devoted to the selection and training of these men is critical. A potential candidate can easily be put off by the recruiter's hidden messages. The response of the recruiter, both in substance and in manner, may be the single most meaningful answer the potential recruit will get to his unasked questions: Am I really welcome in this organization? Is there a career here where I can find meaningful and ego-enhancing work?

To secure a good recruitment team the city needs a committed administrator who sincerely intends to solve the problems of implementation, and the man he selects to head the recruiting program must fall into one of two categories. Preferably, the personal values of the task force chief will coincide with the stated goal; failing that, the individual selected will be able to exert all efforts to achieve the stated goal no matter what his personal feelings may be. Some police departments in the United States may have to settle for the latter alternative.

Normally, a recruitment program follows these approximate guidelines: an announcement of a forthcoming examination, accompanied by publicity in the form of informational materials in public places; visits to schools and colleges; and advertisements in the media. The recruitment of blacks requires extraordinary measures, such as those taken in Washington, D.C.: extensive publicity in the black press and radio, mobile units with loudspeakers, and police exhibits manned by black policemen in black neighborhoods. In Philadelphia the police department ran a telethon and even offered to send a car out to pick up interested applicants. Everything should be done that is likely to have an effect on the resistance to police that has accumulated over the years.

Not public relations techniques but substantive issues will be most important to a successful effort. The first involves the selection procedure itself. What is the process whereby a candidate becomes a policeman? We must review the written examination and see to it that oral interviews are not structured in a way that leaves black candidates disadvantaged. What about the nature and extent of the character investigation? What about the use of the polygraph? What appeal procedures are available to candidates who have been disqualified? From beginning to end, procedures and structures of the selection process need to be revised to better determine the black candidate's ability to do the job. Detroit has instituted a test of a person's ability to learn; it also identifies basic personal attributes (e.g., the ability to operate under stress and the ability to make decisions quickly while under pressure) that are valuable in police work but are not necessarily brought to light by tests that measure writing skills or facility with language. Although still too new to be evaluated, the test has already shown a lower rate of failure for minority group applicants than the written test it replaced.

The same comprehensive reexamination and revision must be undertaken with respect to job assignments. We need to create the atmosphere that everybody, across the board, has equal opportunity for assignments. That means, if necessary, building into police structures the opportunity to learn skills that may be requisites for choice assignments.

The definition of desirable assignments changes from time to time. In New York City in the 1950s, when blacks were relegated to the black areas, the feeling was generated that if blacks were good enough to be cops they were good enough to work anywhere in the city. Then-Commissioner Stephen Kennedy began to assign blacks to motorcycle duty, where they had never been used before, and to traffic and detective divisions, where there had been only a handful. More recently, however, black policemen are becoming increasingly interested in serving the black community. This should not only be allowed, it should be encouraged. One of the unique attributes of the police profession is that the greatest discretion in encounters between the public and the police occurs at the level of the beat patrolman. Black input with a service orientation is most desirable at this level of interaction and will be swiftly read by the black community as a signal of the determination of the department to increase its responsiveness to local needs.

Black applicants should understand that recruit selection has been based on qualities having reference not to power, authority, and repression but to service, consensus, and community protection. The same service assumptions must underlie the training received by the black recruit. And finally, when he receives his appointment, he must be free from discrimination with respect to promotion and job assignments; and as a symbolic "protector" of the black community, he must be allowed to contribute to the law enforcement policy-formulating system. Only under these conditions can the recruitment promise of effectuating change carry credibility among young blacks.

13. The Police Condition

The foregoing account of programs and our speculations on possible new directions are submitted against the background of a tradition in which the public view of the policeman has not been notably approbatory. We nevertheless believe that the proposed evolution of police role and of the public's perception of the police is a reasonable development—indeed, compared with other institutional changes taking place throughout the nation, almost an inevitable one. The evolution can be described simply as being in the direction of democracy. We are attempting to define the social, organizational, and psychological circumstances out of which a truly democratic police can be born.

Historically, the American police have been responsive primarily to the needs of political organizations and the concentrations of power they represented. Political influence in police organizations has been very great, especially with respect to appointments, promotions, and transfers. In the nineteenth century, the election of a new mayor might signal change in a police department from top to bottom. The connection between the police and the political system could not have been more intimate. With the advent of the civil service merit system, this connection became considerably more tenuous. The politician no longer has effective control over police appointments, promotions, and transfers. These now come under the jurisdiction of the police administrator. By and large, however, the police continue to function as though the earlier relationship remained in force. The police still think and act as though they were responsible only to the internal police system, through its hierarchical structure to the chief administrator, and through him to the elected officials who hold political power.

One effect of this attitude is that the typical patrolman never realizes that he ought to seek approval for his activities from within the community in which he works. On the contrary, it is impressed on him from the beginning by his peers that his primary responsibility is to the police subculture. This fosters an alienation from the community which is underscored by the most dominant characteristics of the police subculture: secrecy, cynicism, isolation, and a willingness to exercise authority—to the point of unauthorized violence—purely on behalf of police goals.

Seventy-four policemen in an industrial city of about 150,000 were asked: "When do you think a policeman is justified in roughing a man up?" Two out of every three officers gave as their primary response essentially extra-legal justifications for the use of force—to punish disrespect for the police, to obtain information, to abuse the person of "hardened criminals," and finally, "when you know the man is guilty." Fewer than 10 percent offered as justification for violence a legitimate reason, "to make an arrest."[1] During a recent two-year period in New York City, 71 percent of all authenticated incidents of police brutality resulted from "defense of authority."[2]

Another study, undertaken by the Center for Research on Social Organization, sent 36 volunteers out in Boston, Chicago, and Washington to sit in patrol cars and otherwise monitor booking and lockup procedures in high-crime precincts. Among the findings were the following:

- During a seven-week period there were 37 cases of force being used improperly.

- One third of all observations of undue force occurred in station houses.

- Police administrators tended to be more incensed because officers had behaved improperly in front of observers than by the behavior itself.

- Improper use of force is no more common against black citizens than against white, but it is without exception directed toward the deviant, the dispossessed, and notably the citizens of the lower class.[3]

As the author of the report, Albert J. Reiss, Jr., points

out, the type of behavior that citizens regard as abuse of authority by the police is considered by the police no more than legitimate means toward their goal of law enforcement:

> What citizens mean by police brutality covers the full range of police practices. These practices, contrary to the impression of many civil-rights activists, are not newly devised to deal with Negroes in our urban ghettos. They are ways in which the police have traditionally behaved in dealing with certain citizens, particularly those in the lower classes. The most common of these practices are
>
> • the use of profane and abusive language;
>
> • commands to move on or get home;
>
> • stopping and questioning people on the street or searching them and their cars;
>
> • threats to use force if not obeyed;
>
> • prodding with a nightstick or approaching with a pistol;
>
> • the actual use of physical force or violence itself.[4]

As Reiss notes, such treatment was experienced by succeeding waves of immigrants to the United States, beginning with the Irish and the Germans in the mid-1800s, then the Eastern and Southern Europeans at the turn of the century, and now, especially, indigenous blacks and Puerto Ricans. This behavior is less a function of police prejudice—though that is unquestionably present—than of two main factors: the absence of police accountability except to the police system itself, and the assumption on the part of the police that the public is the enemy.

In Westley's study, 73 percent of police respondents felt that the public was "against the police, hates the police," and only 12 percent felt that the public "likes the police."[5]

In another study, 43 percent of police polled felt that the people in their neighborhood had little or no respect for police. Almost half the officers polled indicated their belief that the least respected of nine occupations on the questionnaire was that of police.[6]

Much of the pressure that compels a policeman to destroy goodwill in abusive language and behavior comes from his belief that his supply of goodwill is low in the community anyway. And of course the more he behaves in that manner, the more likely he is to be correct in his view. He has created a self-fulfilling prophesy.

Certainly what the rookie learns when he arrives on the job—not only from street experiences but also through advice from older officers—does nothing to lessen the situation. He soon discovers (perhaps with a shock) that his primary responsibility is not to the public at large but to his fellow officers. He is initiated into a subculture that highly values in-group secrecy, the maintenance of "respect," and a laissez-faire attitude toward one's colleagues' human failings. Experienced officers, in Westley's study, advised that a rookie should (in decreasing order of frequency cited): "listen to the older man, keep his mouth shut, don't be cocky or an eager beaver, respect the older man's feelings and cooperate, don't be a stool pigeon, do his job, find out the bad ones (stool pigeons), remember that police work is common sense and mind his own business."[7] Clearly, the policeman sees his authority figures (sergeants, lieutenants, captains) as being potentially inimical to his interests. Unfortunately, his experience with the police hierarchy often fails to

educate him for alternatives to the authoritarian presence—which induces the very problems an authoritarian
presence hopes to overcome.

In this respect, the role of the police administrator is
a crucial one. In many instances, the rank-and-file police
officer interprets the positive community relations positions of a chief or a commissioner as being "political";
that is, as being at best an accommodation with the politics of the times and at worst a yielding to political pressure to make political concessions that erode respect for
law enforcement. Many police administrators, however,
hold basically authoritarian views, and their departments
reflect the chief's distaste for and resistance to any
changes that alter the classic authoritarian model of
police behavior. The numerous other administrators, who
clearly recognize the need for change, face a twofold
problem. First, they must formulate that change in a way
that relieves the patrolman of at least some of the trau-
matic encounters he experiences on the street. Second,
they must implement it in a way that impresses on police
middle management that they mean what they say. In
addition, they must deal with the tendency of the officers
to feel defensive (and defenseless) because of the actual
or implied criticism of their "natural" way of functioning
and its replacement by another way which, they fear,
means that the chief has joined the enemy—that is, the
civilian.

"The theme of an enemy public that threatens and
criticizes binds the policeman's group to isolation and
secrecy," writes Westley. "It is an occupational directive,
a rule of thumb, the sustenance and the core of
meanings."[8]

The notion of the policeman as a law-enforcing dis-
ciplinarian who intrudes on the citizen's liberty and is

therefore to be considered an enemy and an alien is one which the police themselves should want to discourage. On the whole, however, the pressure for a change in the police role which has come from the community has been resisted by the police. This is probably due to the inability of police administrators to visualize for themselves a role that would be different but would not, at the same time, diminish their power. Clearly, this fear is based on reluctance to relinquish the classical view of the police connection to politics, to elected officials, and to community power bases that lie within an elite component rather than within the community at large.

One consequence of this attitude is an unwillingness to forego the part of the police identity which rests on and is maintained by the semimilitary aura. The police is an organization geared to respond to emergency, even though most of its work is not emergency work. Police are trained, equipped, and maintained on the model of a standing army. We know that crimes are committed by people who have both the inclination and the opportunity, and that an authoritarian presence can serve to deprive them of the opportunity, thus dampening their inclination. Most studies indicate, however, that maintaining such a presence forms a very small portion of the police effort, although it continues to be virtually all the police identity. Moreover, the public seems to accept this view of the police uncritically. People tend to believe that if you arrest enough people, the problem will be solved. In most instances, people will say: We want the police to make more arrests. What they mean is: We want the police to help us solve our problems. And to solve those problems, the police as a semimilitaristic bureaucracy have been (and will continue to be) largely ineffective.

Having been an organization that responds to crisis, the police must now learn to become an out-reach body, entering the community not only in response to crisis but at a time and in a way that circumvents crisis. Instead of entering the community with force, they must acquire expertise in community conflict management that will obviate the need for force. The patrolman functioning as part of a semimilitaristic bureaucracy has neither the training nor the skills nor the role image to properly perform the work described. Among police generally, there has been too little employee participation in decision making. The patrolman's experience has been entirely that of he who obeys orders, not at all that of he who contributes to the solution of problems. Even though more and more police precincts are trying to develop dialogues between officers and their "superiors," the rank and file still have no functional control over their professional lives and are thus deprived of a primary source of self-respect. It is little wonder that by and large policemen are unreceptive to the idea that the people ought to have a meaningful voice in their governance—including, of course, the nature and extent of the police service they receive.

A recent Rand Institute study of police in New York City revealed that a disproportionately high number of better-educated officers terminated their service. One-third of the college-educated recruits who joined the New York force were found to have left within ten years.

The data suggests that many men who represent the Department's view of a desirable candidate, especially college-educated men, will have shorter tenure than the average officer unless the Department consciously attempts to determine the source of

dissatisfaction among such officers and modifies the
personnel policies accordingly.[9]

We believe that the undemocratic factors just mentioned
are likely to be among the reasons for a well-educated
policeman's negative view of his job. Indeed, they are
likely to be significant regardless of educational level
achieved. Most policemen have no meaningful voice in
their governance.

If we are to arrest and disperse the pall of citizen dis-
content that hangs over the police as an institution, by
effecting the changes outlined here, we must begin at the
beginning, questioning our concepts of what it means
to be a police officer in the 1970s and beyond.

Part Three
Community Police

14. Team Policing

Some of the programs we have described in previous chapters have worked very well; others have been less satisfactory. They are all worth trying, if local circumstances suggest that they would be effective. Yet however useful such procedures might be, they alone will not solve the problem of police and community in the United States in the 1970s.

Individual programs, no matter how well intentioned or earnestly pursued, will not change the basic, unfortunate

149

police–community condition—namely, that the police and the community are not partners in the effort to prevent crime and to maintain order.

Some communities suffer more than others from this situation, and some police departments suffer more than others from citizen antipathy and alienation, but nowhere, it seems, do police and community enjoy a condition of mutual trust and respect. We know of one qualified exception—Holyoke, Massachusetts—which is discussed in another chapter.

Some of the reasons for poor police–community relations are clearly beyond the scope of police intervention. The police cannot and should not be expected to suffer public disapprobation for social conditions that are more properly the responsibility of others. The police must not allow themselves to stand in for real or symbolic failures of the social system, and they must not be utilized in a way that incarnates those very flaws.

Lawbreakers are not necessarily criminals. The police must realize that in our time, more and more people who are not motivated by antisocial impulses are breaking laws. Many people who would not otherwise be thought of as "criminal" will break the law to preserve a valued social custom, to maintain personal identity, or to still the qualms of conscience. A Puerto Rican "loiters" and refuses to move on because as far as he is concerned, "loitering" is done by everybody who wants to take part in the life of his community. A black man refuses to respond to a police officer who speaks to him discourteously. A middle-class college student demonstrates against the presence on campus of a government official to whose acts or policies he is utterly opposed. These individuals are not criminals in the classic sense, and a police determined to see itself primarily as a law enforcement mechanism will find itself ever more alienated from all such manifestations of the day's social ferment. Suppose, however, that the police role is thought of primarily as one of conflict management or the maintenance of order in the community, with only a small percentage of time actually devoted to law enforcement (as is actually the case). Then the department no longer has to confront situations like those just described in an adversary manner. And with few exceptions, as soon as the police commence this reorientation, the community can be expected to make a comparable shift in its attitude toward the police.

"The principal objectives of modern urban policing should be the maintenance of public order," writes William A. Westley. "To achieve this objective, the police must have the cooperation of citizens, be trained in skills eliciting such cooperation and be given a relationship to the community which breeds trust and confidence."[1]

In our view, the police can achieve such a relationship to the community only if they have first determined that they want it and have taken steps to create a structure that will encourage it. One very promising structure is the team police concept.

The team policing idea originated during the late 1940s in Aberdeen, Scotland, as a patrol experiment. The idea was to replace traditional beats with a larger district, to be patrolled by a team of constables under the command of a sergeant who had sufficient discretionary authority to adjust patrolling methods and administrative disposition of the men in his command to suit the needs of the district. The idea spread to Salford, England, in 1950, and to the United States in the early 1960s, when it made an experimental appearance in Syracuse, New York, where former New York City Police Commissioner Patrick Murphy had just become Syracuse police chief. As did the British programs, the Syracuse plan emphasized the provision of necessary police services, but it also contained a new element appropriate to the times—the participation of the community. The emphasis in Syracuse was on law enforcement and crime prevention, but certain structural elements suggested Murphy's awareness that during the tumultuous 1960s police in the United States were obliged to recognize the need for public involvement in the criminal justice system, and particularly the police operation. Elements in the program also prefigured the idea of increased "accountability," both for middle managers and beat patrolmen, which was prominent in Murphy's programs for New York City's police, notably the neighborhood police teams. Other police programs around the country also have contained these elements, among them Detroit's Beat Commander System and the Los Angeles Basic "A" Car Plan.

The first of these programs, Detroit's Beat Commander System, was inaugurated experimentally in the high-crime Tenth Precinct at the beginning of 1970. Like all similar projects, the Beat Commander System represented a return to the decentralized, highly personalized police service that can only be provided by the beat patrolman who is permanently in contact with his own assigned area. For many years it was police dogma that this personal relationship between the police and the policed was essential to successful policing. As a result of increased department centralization, the shift of foot patrolmen into squad cars, the growing sophistication of law enforcement technology, and other factors (mainly a concern to reduce the temptation of corruption for police who become overfamiliar with their beats), the personal relationship faded and the need for it was deemphasized, with consequences that are all too familiar.

Detroit's Beat Commander System was devised by Murphy when he was director of the Urban Institute's Public Safety Studies; it was begun in Detroit after he went there as commissioner. Murphy and his cooriginator, Peter B. Bloch of the Urban Institute, explained the intent of the system and the underlying theory as follows:

> First, the small ratio of police to citizens makes it impossible for the police alone to deter crime. They cannot be visible or nearby at all times and in all places. For maximum crime prevention, therefore, a potential criminal must begin to know that every resident of an area is a potential assistant to the police.
>
> Second, good community relations does not result from the public relations efforts of the police department headquarters or of some specialized unit or bureau under the chief, useful as these efforts may be. Rather, good community relations is the product of all the various encounters between citizens and police personnel. Thus, the individual officer must understand that his actions will affect the amount and degree of cooperation—or opposition—he will receive.[2]

Under the Beat Commander System a police team of approximately two dozen men, led by a sergeant, was responsible for police service on a Detroit beat—roughly two squad cars' territory—with a population of about 15,000 citizens.

Several assumptions lay behind the formation of this team: that increased police familiarity with a specific neighborhood produces improved police service, that increased personal responsibility enhances police self-image, and that improved police service of a nonpunitive nature (medical, educational, and vocational referrals) leads to the kind of citizen cooperation with the police that cannot develop within the framework of an alienated, authoritarian police. Preliminary data indicate that all these assumptions are correct. More crimes were reported in the experimental precinct, and there was appreciably improved officer job attitude (as indexed by reduced sick leave averages), speedier police service, and widespread community acceptance of the program.

By May 1971 the city was to have expanded the project to five additional beats which, with five control beats patrolled in the traditional fashion, would have provided a more comprehensive, year-long, augmented experimental model. By the end of the year, however, the program had been discontinued, and John F. Nichols, Murphy's successor as Detroit Police Commissioner, describing himself as a "realist" and a "cop" whose major concern was crime control and prevention, said, "We could find little of value in the neighborhood team concept."[3]

Murphy, commenting on data indicating an increase in arrests since the program was discontinued, acknowledged that a motorized police may make more arrests but often such arrests do not lead to prosecutions. He continued:

> The value of nonprosecution arrests has to be weighed against public acceptance. Many police are afraid or resentful of strange police officers, who come in to sweep their streets clean. Often, that kind of procedure ruins some of the good that has been accomplished in a neighborhood.[4]

As with the Detroit model, the New York City Neighborhood Police Team emphasizes the responsibility of the local commander, within policy guidelines, to control crime in a manner and with methods that pragmatically suit his own area; it also takes into account the needs of the citizens of the area. The rigidity and impersonality of a high bureaucratic structure are modified in favor of the more flexible, decentralized model.

The New York City program commenced operations January 1, 1971, in the 77th Precinct in the Bedford-Stuyvesant district of Brooklyn. The area chosen was a residential and business community accounting for 16 percent of the crime in the precinct. The program was later instituted in similar high-crime precincts in the Bronx, Queens, and Manhattan, and many of the city's precincts, as of this writing, have one or more teams. According to Murphy:

> The key to the Neighborhood Police Team program is the faith we have in the ability of patrolmen and lower-level superior officers to shoulder more responsibility. Under the Neighborhood Police Team Program, a sergeant will be permanently assigned to a precinct sector and will be responsible, on a 24-hour-a-day basis, for that sector. He will have discretion in utilizing patrol resources to the best advantage within the sector territory and will have increased flexibility to determine his own working hours and those of his men. He will become the "Neighborhood Chief of Police."[5]

The team commander is given to understand that service functions are as important as law enforcement functions. The commander and his men are encouraged to provide assistance to the people of the community, making job referrals for the unemployed, medical referrals for the ill or the addicted, and performing similar liaison services between the people and social agencies. The area that the team polices is indeed its area of responsibility, and that responsibility is shared by each officer of the team.

"If he does his job well," Murphy says, "he makes friends in the community, he helps people who are in trouble, he helps others to avoid trouble, he earns confidence for himself and his department, and most of all he makes a positive contribution to the fight against crime."[6]

The Basic "A" Car Plan, a program similar in intent, if not in structure, has been operating in Los Angeles since April, 1970. This concept emphasizes community meetings and continuity of police presence to increase the patrolman's knowledge of the people and the area of his responsibility. Los Angeles Chief E. M. Davis has discussed the program as follows:

> The fundamental objective of police work is to help society prevent crime and to deter people from committing crime. . . . The way police administrators have historically deployed policemen has created a situation directly opposite from that necessary to get the job of prevention and deterrence accomplished. No one is kept very long on any assignment, radio car districts are changed on different days of the week, officers are rotated frequently. Each of these actions was designed to answer a problem, but the problems they created far outstrip the value of the solutions they offer.[7]

To answer the newly created problems—mainly those produced by police alienation from the citizens they serve—the Basic Car Plan assigns a radio car team of nine men to cover three watches in a Basic Car district. As with earlier British experiments and to a certain extent the New York Neighborhood Team concept, the lead officer of the "A" Car Team has flexibility in determining police needs in the district. He is responsible for maintaining a profile folder of the district, containing such material as data and maps on area crime problems and names of

wanted suspects. To a great extent, the folder is kept
current by the feedback provided by community meetings.

A police officer from Holyoke, Massachusetts, himself
part of an experimental team police program, visited the
Los Angeles Basic Car Plan units and produced a report
that included the following comments:

> . . . The plan met with resistance from the Police
> Department in the beginning but is now being ac-
> cepted by those not in the Plan. The value of the
> Plan seems to be in the fact that people are meeting
> the Policemen in their areas for perhaps the first
> time and are able to talk over a problem with a per-
> son instead of an official voice over the phone. . . .
> I spoke to one of the men in the Plan alone and he
> was delighted with the Plan, but would like to do
> more investigating; but with their present setup
> there is not time for them to go farther. . . . He re-
> ported that they do not have any more trouble in
> minority areas when an arrest is made than they do
> in any other part of the City.[8]

Underscoring the critical community relations thrust of
the Basic Car plan is the accountability of each patrol
division's Community Relations Officer for the success
of the Basic Car Plan in his division. (In Los Angeles there
are 17 divisions. The lieutenant in charge is responsible,
in turn, to his division commander.) Under the charge of
the Community Relations Officer, each division has a
Basic Car Plan Coordinator who aids in special program
preparation, format, development, film and brochure pro-
curement, and Basic Car district meeting publicity for all
Basic Car Teams on all watches. An integral part of the
plan is organizing the community to meet and effectively
communicate with officers on the subject of police problems in the district.

From Chief Davis's own assessment of the program,

there has been an improvement in the police–community relationship and, perhaps as a consequence, there have been "miraculous attitudinal changes in the officers" taking part in the "A" Car idea. Chief Davis told a convention of the International Association of Chiefs of Police that the program had convinced him that police–community relations problems must be dealt with at the grass-roots level—that is, in friendly encounters on the street between the officer and the citizen. The Basic Car Plan, Davis said, was "putting the police and the people closer together month by month." [9]

The policy in the Los Angeles Police Department is to judge all officers partly by their community relations performance. For the 810 officers of the Basic Car Plan, now operating in 90 districts, the community relations factor is even more significant, since a critical element of the program is the monthly community meeting held in public schools in the various districts.

At some community relations meetings the police and the citizens seem to be operating from different sides of the street, and racial antagonisms are aired. The Basic Car Plan meetings, however, are concerned solely with police problems and with questions relating to improving police performance and developing more effective means of crime prevention. The police team and the citizens are assumed to be partners in a joint enterprise, and the meeting is run not by ranking officers from outside the district but by the Basic Car Team's lead officer. All the officers of the Basic Car Team attend, and those off duty at the time are compensated for their overtime hours. Thus responsibility for community cooperation is brought down to the lowest level in the police hierarchy —the level of policy execution.

Following a general session, the meetings are divided into discussion workshops with each officer of the team acting as a workshop chairman. In addition to general discussions of the current crime profile in the district, there are presentations by resource specialists (detectives, narcotics officers), and citizens are given the opportunity to bring pertinent matters to the attention of the officers. If they cannot deal with the problem immediately, they try to arrive at a solution as soon as possible. This exercise develops in the man on the beat—the man at the enforcement level—the same involvement, dedication, and accountability formerly expected only of higher ranking officers.

Consequently, it is heartening to discover that these young officers have come to change their attitudes regarding minority members, the idea of community relations work, and the concept of a police officer who is personally responsible for the quality of the police service on his beat.

Community involvement in the "A" Car Plan has been extensive: during 1970, a total of almost 80,000 persons attended Basic Car Plan community meetings. "Interesting presentations, refreshments, and fellowship encourage consistent participation," the department brochure dryly notes.[10] It is clear, however, that no amount of refreshments alone could have accounted for the "miraculous" attitudinal changes on the part of the officers. The two critical elements were the decrease in emotional distance between the individual officer and those he serves, and the resultant increase in the policeman's own sense of autonomy, responsibility, and personal worth.

Affording the individual police officer a greater opportunity to exercise his initiative and skills creates a higher level of personal motivation. Such motivation is essential to the success of neighborhood police programs and it is also one of their most visible and most valuable benefits. A police officer whose judgment is respected is more likely to make mature judgments. A police officer whose self-respect is enhanced will be more receptive to the idea that the citizen must be dealt with respectfully. On the other hand, a police officer lacking power will not be inclined to appreciate expressed needs for black power, community power, or any other sort of power; yet a police officer who participates in policy making, at least insofar as his own functioning is concerned, can relate to the community's desire to share in the solution to its own crime problems.

It cannot be said too often that a police officer deprived of a meaningful role in the life of the community, and lacking a positive self-image, cannot function responsibly and cannot provide the police service that the times demand. Thus any program that fosters attitudinal changes, to say nothing of "miraculous" ones, deserves respectful notice. And on a more concrete basis, Chief Davis cites statistics indicating that public complaints against the department have decreased 12 percent.

In the few documented cases we have, the aforementioned positive effects on the performance and on the self-image of the police officer have been magnified when the scope of the officer's duties has been expanded or when the police role has actually been redefined. A pilot program in Dayton, Ohio, seems to reflect the belief that the ultimate responsibility for police image in a neighborhood resides in the performance of the beat patrolman. The idea is embodied in the team police concept, allied with Dayton's view of the beat patrolman as a generalist/

specialist. The Dayton syllabus on the Team Policing Project defines the generalist/specialist concept as follows:

Today, police are terribly specialized: they have special units—for investigations, traffic control, accident investigation, juvenile aid, community relations, and a wealth of other special activities. Police officers assigned to these specialties rarely receive adequate training to become "book experts" in a technical sense; but over the years, by working at the one identified task, they gain a fairly high degree of competency in a narrow task area.

Such specialization can be destructive to the development of the initiative of field patrol officers. For example, if a beat police officer responds to a traffic accident where a person is injured, in most cities his only responsibility is to aid the sick and injured; the investigation must be left to the accident investigation specialist. The same is true of a great number of situations; for example, if a minor crime is encountered, the detective is called in to investigate and the beat officer goes back on patrol.

With police agencies constantly trying to recruit and utilize college trained men, this type of organization structure does not allow a mature and responsible individual to exercise initiative. Few college graduates would find it attractive, as a job opportunity, to ride around in a marked automobile all day being seen, but not being allowed to follow through on any particular case. And when this occurs, the beat patrol officer cannot be held responsible for what happens on his beat, for all he does is take reports, he doesn't investigate or participate in like matters. Therefore we intend to make the police officer a generalist and allow him to investigate to conclusion all minor crimes, work with area juveniles, investigate those traffic accidents that need investigation, and do related work. He will have complete responsibility for police performance on his beat, except that he will share some responsibility with other members of the "team" of which he is a part.

That is, within a given area, there will be a team of police officers, team leaders, and community service officers. At a given time, a beat will have a team member and a community service officer working there; they will not be on general preventive patrol but will be (1) investigating those crimes that have occurred recently, (2) assisting members of the neighborhood with their problems, (3) answering calls from citizens for service, and (4) assisting the community to maintain order. They, thus, will be task oriented, rather than spending time on preventive patrol. This is the job description of the police generalist.[11]

This passage clearly represents a shift in the emphasis in police priorities from law enforcement to order maintenance and conflict resolutions. The statement of goals is explicit:

Through the Team Policing Program, the Dayton Police Department intends to accomplish three major goals: (1) Test the effectiveness of a generalist approach to police service as opposed to the specialist approach now utilized by all major police organizations. (2) Produce a community-centered police structure that is responsive to neighborhood concerns and understanding of neighborhood life styles, and (3) Alter the bureaucratic structure of the police organization away from the militaristic model towards a neighborhood oriented professional model.

The general overall result of this project should be a demonstration of a new role for the police; that of manager of community conflict.[12]

To change the concept of the police officer's function in the direction indicated, the officers had to be trained to develop additional skills—both technical, such as investigative methods, and personal. The first two weeks of Dayton's four-week training cycle constituted a school in crisis intervention involving specific skills, such as handling a family crisis, and subjective reevaluations by each officer, as well. The instructors were consulting behavioral scientists who had extensive experience in management and psychological training programs, with an emphasis on conflict management. In the third week the trainees took a course either in investigative methods or in such specialized areas as narcotics problems or juvenile aid. During the final training week, all underwent community and neighborhood sensitization.

The project consisted of two teams of eighteen officers each, and the first team went on duty in the pilot district in November 1970. Unlike the rest of the force, the police team was not responsible to the Dayton Police Department central headquarters, although of course Police Chief Igleburger retained authority both as chief and as project director. But responsibility for the police mission in the pilot district lay with the district director, and with the team itself.

To emphasize their uniqueness, members of the police team wore distinctive uniforms, rode in specially marked squad cars, and to further reinforce their remove from the paramilitary police model, grew beards and mustaches if they chose. These far from superficial changes were augmented by the elimination of traditional rank hierarchy, and civilian modes of address were utilized by all team members, the team leaders (formerly sergeants), and the district director (formerly a lieutenant).

To ensure that the community fully understood the change that was being sought—and, more important, to secure maximum citizen cooperation and support—the community's role in the police service was incorporated on several levels. Twelve Community Service Officers were hired from among applicants within the experimental district to undertake certain police service tasks and to assist with sensitive community police problems. A citizens' advisory council, a civilian community coordinator (whose job is to "assist the community in developing defensive security tactics, community concern and community action" and to develop an understanding in the community of the police effort), and a preexistent neighborhood-oriented police auxiliary constituted considerable community involvement. None, however, was more meaningful than the manner in which the police team officers were selected.

All officers participating in the program were volunteers. The district director was selected by a joint neighborhood–police assistance council, which also selected the team members, who then chose their team leaders. All these candidates were subject to the approval of the Director of Police, yet the community's participation in the process of selection—to the extent of being able to reject candidates it found unsuitable—meant that the team police commenced operations with the approbation of at least that portion of the community accessible through community councils.

Finally, an attempt was made to integrate the police officer into the ongoing life of the community:

> It is very important that each police officer be aware of the lifestyles of the neighborhood in which he works; he must understand cultural factors, neighborhood leaders and neighborhood issues. To facilitate such an understanding among police officers assigned to the neighborhood, and to involve the neighborhood in the training process, each officer

accepted for duty in the district (unless waived by
the joint police–neighborhood council) will have to
live with a sponsor family in the neighborhood for
between three and five days. The community assistance council, with the assistance of the community
coordinator, will choose families as "police officer
sponsors." These families will have an officer live
with them for a short period, during which they will
introduce him to their neighborhood. The sponsor
family will be reimbursed for expenses plus a small
honorarium. The police officers will receive a few
extra vacation days and some overtime pay.[13]

In addition to other rewards, each officer participating
in the project received twelve hours of college credit for
the year of his service. Furthermore, to strengthen the
connection between the program and an evolving concept
of the officer's role in the community, it was understood
that evaluation of the officer's performance was to be
based "on success (and quality) of disposition, rather
than quantity of arrests, as now is the case."[14]

For a variety of reasons, the Dayton plan did not operate altogether as envisioned. Since comparable situations
are likely to be encountered in other programs embodying
such substantial change, we must now digress briefly to
separate practice from theory.

The Dayton program evolved initially out of a conference of the National Institute on Police–Community Relations, sponsored in 1967 by Professor Louis Radelet at
Michigan State University. The theme was Alternatives to
Traditional Police Organizations. Patrick Murphy spoke,
and shortly thereafter went to Detroit as Commissioner to
implement his team police concept. John Angell, a sociol-
ogist and former police officer who was then at Kent State
University and later became Director of Training for the
Dayton Police Department, read a paper entitled, "Toward

an Alternative to the Classical Police Organizational Arrangements: A Democratic Model." Afterward, he and Raymond Galvin, who was then on the faculty of the School of Criminal Justice at Michigan State, took the paper to Dayton, where Robert Wasserman, Administrative Assistant to the Chief, reworked it and made it the basis for his proposal for Law Enforcement Assistance Agency funding for the Dayton Team Police concept.

Dayton's was the most comprehensive but by no means the only manifestation of the team police concept in American cities. In addition to the aforementioned programs in New York, Los Angeles, and Detroit, a program resembling Dayton's was instituted in Louisville. This version was developed by Ben Brashears, who had been at Michigan State before becoming a consultant to the Louisville Police Department.

Angell, who went to Louisville to help with the training, now feels that the Kentucky program was improperly implemented and consequently turned into a bureaucratic dead-end. But he is no more satisfied with his own version, in Dayton:

> The program had already gotten under way before I joined the Dayton Police Department, and they were moving in the wrong direction. Mostly in that the program was being run autocratically, which is the opposite of my intention. For one example, storefront buildings were being selected by the Project Director and none of the men were involved in it. He didn't know what the purpose of the storefront was, and couldn't have cared less. We've discovered other flaws: more of a need for continued involvement of citizens, who need to be part of the planning process at the outset, and a need to build in involvement at different policy levels. Training has been pretty much of a failure. I've been down

there raising a fuss, and we've got a new man in there, a lieutenant, who's changing things. There's going to be an improvement.

There are always going to be problems, and whether you think the democratic team police concept is good or bad, we're moving in that direction. I think it's inevitable. We've finished an evaluation of the Team Police Unit in Holyoke, Massachusetts, and we have overwhelming data on certain kinds of opinion change. The officers are happier with it and the people are happier with it.

I'm not surprised. Back in 1967, Professor Radelet wanted alternatives to existing police structures, and a lot of research had already been done. We went through it and tried to compile what made for an effective work group, and all of it seemed to lead in this kind of a direction. The literature of the management field—McGregor, Warren Bennis, and a variety of others—talked about moving in this direction in the business field. The most effective work group is the one where you're concerned about the people in the group and their input, rather than just telling them to do it and expecting that they will.

Studies of World War II American soldiers show that the most effective combat teams were those in which the leadership was chosen by the people in the teams. So our sources were an analysis of existing organizational literature and what we ourselves knew about police departments. The problem was, how to put it all in some kind of structure that you could manage.[15]

15. The Holyoke Model

In the autumn of 1971 a grey-haired, florid-faced, middle-aged man, dressed in grey flannels and blue blazer, was walking along the street in the Flats, an area of Holyoke, Massachusetts, that contains one of the two ghetto wards. As he approached a group of Puerto Rican children at play, a little boy looked up and said, with a friendly grin, "Hello, officer."

"I want you to notice two things," the man said a moment later to his companion. "First, he recognized the outfit I'm wearing as a police uniform. Second, he wasn't afraid of it."

The companion had indeed noted both points. Captain George Burns, Jr., the police officer in slacks and blazer, was unable to repress his pleasure. Burns is Project Director of Holyoke's Team Police Unit. He believes that team police have altered for the good the relationship between the black and the Spanish-speaking minorities of Ward One and the police who serve them. And he receives strong support from data compiled by John Angell, Raymond Galvin, and Michael O'Neill, of the University of California in Los Angeles, who evaluated the one-year experimental model.

Ward One was a notorious high-crime area before the team police appeared. From the time of their arrival in December 1970, through 1971, however, there was only one mugging in the ward. We know that in most police–minority group encounters, the two sides approach each other as adversaries, and the militant, antipolice atmosphere deepens perceptibly each time the police appear. Yet since the initiation of the experimental model of team police, this has not been the case in Holyoke's Ward One. In 1970 there were 70 assaults logged on police officers within the ward. Many were minor (e.g., in connection with resistance to arrest), but some were serious. One officer was stabbed, another narrowly missed a skull fracture when a flowerpot was thrown at him, and a third was shot in the stomach. Yet the following year, with the team police, there were no assaults.

Despite the clear service orientation of the program, moreover, police administrators dedicated to the law enforcement view of police work are unable to fault it. According to Deputy Police Chief Francis O'Connell:

> They're making more arrests in the Flats than
> they've ever made, yet this year [1972] was cool.
> The previous year, the same area was a pressure
> cooker. We had tremendous problems with the
> minorities there. The people were reluctant to come
> downtown to headquarters, there were frequent
> confrontations and assaults on police. One officer
> was knifed four times. Another one, Patrolman
> Stephen Donaghue, was shot in the stomach.[1]

Holyoke's Ward One is in many respects a typical inner-
city ghetto. The ward's 4700 residents (about 50 percent
of them black and Puerto Rican) are isolated from the rest
of the city by a series of canals that completely encircle
the area, thus dramatizing the psychosocial situation of
the residents. About 20 percent of the ward's families live
on less than $3000 a year. Almost 30 percent live in sub-
standard housing. Also known as the Paper City, Holyoke
was the first planned industrial community in the United
States, and the legacy of the industrial revolution of a
previous century is constricted streets, outmoded housing, a lack of open space, congestion, and obsolete
factories.

Ward One is the Model Neighborhood of the Model
Cities program, which aims to improve the quality of life
in the inner cities in such areas as housing, education,
social services, and police functions. Until 1972, the director of the Model Cities program in Holyoke was Reverend
Henry Ramsey, a former chaplain at Smith College. Ramsey believes that neither police administration nor any
other establishment structures have kept pace with human
development since the nineteenth century:

> Look at the structures decision makers create for
> people who are not decision makers down in Ward
> One, in the Model Neighborhood. Look at the place.

It's completely surrounded by moats, the canals, by
big industrial buildings all around, very reminiscent
of a medieval wall. Two big church steeples which
are very reminiscent of a medieval town—a well-
ordered town—you can see the positions of power
there. In the nineteenth century, when the Irish people lived there, a bell rang in the morning, told
everybody when to get up, when to report to work,
when to come home to lunch, when to come back,
and their entire life was structured physically and
temporally by walls and moats and bells and square
streets. That's one of the problems in the Model
Neighborhood. We're living in a time that doesn't
structure life like that, and people have mobility.
The physical parts don't fit what the people do.[2]

One consequence of increased mobility for the Flats
was a new wave of immigration from Puerto Rico. Pre-
dictably, the area became rife with intergroup conflicts
between whites, blacks, and Spanish-speaking people,
and it was soon the focus of hostile relations between the
police and the community. The language barrier was particularly serious, for not infrequently a Puerto Rican who
called the police for assistance would himself be assumed
by the officers for assistance to the call to be the *cause* of
the disturbance, and would be arrested because he
couldn't explain the situation.

The social climate in this high-crime area was increasingly marked by acts of violence, culminating in the
shooting of Patrolman Donaghue. "It happened just before
midnight on May 16, 1970," Donaghue recalls. "On our
first sweep through the Flats in the cruiser there was a
group of fellows flagrantly drinking beer in front of us. So
we said, 'Hey, we told you guys no drinking in the streets,
how many times we have to tell you?' So it's 'No speak
English,' you know?"[3]

That this interchange led, a few moments later, to the shooting of Donaghue, is a clear indication of the tension, mistrust, and lack of communication between the police and the people of the community. The gunman ran off, and Donaghue's partner took him to the hospital, where he received 15 pints of blood and 7 pints of plasma. Those who stayed behind spread the word that a Puerto Rican had been shot by the police, and there was a minor riot that night, with windows smashed and a number of fires started.

The blacks, the Puerto Ricans, and the nativist French-speaking whites of Ward One, who had supplanted the immigrant Irish in the area, were dissatisfied with the police service, but for different reasons. The blacks and Puerto Ricans complained of brutality, indifference, and lack of concern, while the whites spoke of a lack of protection and police permissiveness toward minorities. The police themselves had come to refer to Ward One as "the combat zone." The climate was just short of incendiary. The Board of Aldermen demanded that Mayor Taupier "do something," and he in turn authorized Jack Goss, the Evaluations Director for the Model Cities Agency, to come up with a program.

Goss, a former police commissioner in Springfield, Massachusetts, had already been thinking about the problem. And so had Captain Burns, who was then the department's police–community relations officer. Burns and Tom Sweeney, a young man from the Lower Pioneer Valley Planning Commission, had been trying to figure out how to attract federal funds to the area; they proposed a Team Police Unit, based loosely on recommendations of the President's Commission on Law Enforcement and Administration of Justice. Goss contributed his ideas, and the final program evolved when the Team Police officers themselves organized the unit on the basis of the proposal that was forwarded to the Law Enforcement Assistance Administration. The LEAA contributed $40,000 to augment a Model Cities grant of $129,000 and the city's allocation to the police budget of $130,000.

Goss, a former investigator with the Massachusetts Attorney General's office and a member of a board of police commissioners bearing administrative responsibility for the conduct of a 400-man police department, is a registered Republican who considers himself a traditionalist. Nevertheless, he realized that nothing less than radical innovation could shatter the impasse between the police and the minority communities of Holyoke. As Goss saw it, the first step had to be made by the police:

> It was obvious to me that police in the United States haven't demonstrated more than limited effectiveness in controlling crime, in dealing with violent dissent and disorder, in improving community relations, and in providing general services to the community. It seemed to me that for police to improve their effectiveness in these areas they had first and foremost to develop a satisfactory role conception to govern their performance. That means the actual day-to-day operation of a particular officer in a particular day. They also had to get the community to help them define police priority through some kind of meaningful dialogue. In other words, briefly, they had to understand that their primary task is the management of community conflict, not simply law enforcement.[4]

The proposal sent to LEAA envisioned attaining three primary goals through the team police concept:

1. Demonstrating the effectiveness of the generalist

approach to the police officer's duties and role within the police structure.

2. Creating a service-oriented, community-centered, accountable police, operating within organizational parameters that permit the officers to be truly responsive to citizen input.

3. Altering the bureaucratic structure of police away from the centralized, hierarchical, semimilitaristic model.

Thus the police was to derive its authority not from an administrator responsible only to the sources of political power, but from having defined itself in conjunction with the people it served.

When the funds arrived, the department named Captain Burns as project director and sent out a call for volunteers. Burns and Goss gave a series of orientations to the rank and file. Burns candidly admits that these speeches emphasized a variety of incentives to make the program look as good as possible to potential volunteers:

> It's natural for people to fear change. So I emphasized such things as freedom from central control, an attractive uniform of their own choosing, no roll call, the right to make their own hours, increased self-supervision, and the like. In addition to the autonomy, there would be extra pay and academic credit at Holyoke Community College while on duty. Most of all, though, I emphasized that they would be doing more interesting work.[5]

Twenty-five men responded to the call, among them Patrolman Donaghue, only recently out of the hospital.

Burns selected seventeen men, including two sergeants, to put through the training cycle.

After a 12-hour orientation in the philosophy and purpose of team policing, volunteers received a 120-hour course, designed and administered by the Holyoke Community College Law Enforcement Program, emphasizing police investigative skills and conflict management skills. Undertaken by an independent contractor, the main course consisted of an intensive one-week program supplemented by weekly 2-hour follow-up sessions during the early months of the operational phase. Commented Goss:

> The implicit, and sometimes explicit, assumption of all the training was a change in the conception of the police officer's role. Change that and all else follows naturally. So we commenced with Angell's idea of the beat patrolman as a responsible generalist/specialist out to serve the community's total police needs in such a way as to gain their approval and support.[6]

Two parallel organizations were created to serve the community's needs. One, the Community Relations Council, consisted of six civilians and three police officers, including the Team Police Project Director, who served *ex officio*. The council was primarily responsible for formulating programs to enhance police–community relations in the ward and for anticipating potential law-enforcement problems. The other organization, the Crime and Delinquency Task Force, was composed of sixteen persons representing a demographic profile of the area— four residents each of the French, Irish, Spanish-speaking, and black communities. The four members of each group were distributed in juvenile, young adult, adult, and senior citizen age categories. This body worked with the Police Team in an advisory capacity to help define the community's policy toward policing and to act as a forum in which cross-cultural conflicts within the ward could be aired and resolved.

To provide police an uninterrupted line of communication to these bodies, which met at two- or three-week intervals, the position of neighborhood liaison specialist was added to the project director's staff. This high-level position was filled by a civilian who represented to the project director the views of the two citizen committees on a continuing basis.

The program also included four community service officers, chosen from within the neighborhood, to serve along with the sworn officers in the team. The community's voice in the determination of the police service it received in Ward One was obviously a strong one.

If a visionary for social change were to redesign his local police he might come up with the following scenario. First engage a small group of volunteers to take on the law-enforcement and order-maintenance tasks in a community, urging them to consult with the community in determining the nature and extent of crime in the area. Next discard the traditional uniform and put the officers into a readily identifiable outfit (of their own choosing) that carries no militaristic or repressive connotations. Eliminate rank within the force, and give all the officers an equal vote, regardless of former police rank, not only on administrative procedures but on policy and disciplinary matters as well. Then provide the force with salaried civilian aides from the neighborhood to act as liaison and as interpreters, if necessary. Back up the unit with social service agencies open 24 hours a day for specialist referrals of a social or psychiatric nature. Place the police in a readily accessible and if possible inviting location—say, a storefront—and firmly advise them that they are there to serve the community. Finally, impress on the officers that they have complete responsibility for police performance on the beat.

Visionary though it might be, the foregoing description fits the police unit that moved into its storefront headquarters in Holyoke's Ward One in December 1970 and commenced operations as the Team Police Unit. The beat patrolman had complete responsibility for police performance and was allowed to pursue investigations to conclusion, except for major crimes like murder, which called for the higher specialization of headquarters detectives (however, there were no murders). Moreover, the patrolman came to be a community resource in dealing with such problems as juvenile delinquency, narcotics problems, and family crises.

All members of the Team Police Unit handled beat problems of a generalist nature, but an officer could call on other members of the team for more specialized assistance, much as a family physician might consult an internist. As Burns pointed out:

> Different men have different skills. One loves fingerprinting, another loves photography, a third has developed fantastic rapport with young blacks. The unit has a meeting every couple of weeks to work out differences, and it came up at one meeting that this officer was playing basketball with black kids on duty. Other officers were complaining. So I said that in my opinion what he was doing was good police work and that nobody complained when the other fellow spent duty time in the photo lab. Everybody saw the connection, and they agreed.[7]

The police unit, in this view of its responsibilities, becomes a task-oriented work team. Preventive patrol is eliminated, and in place of motorized officers making random passes through an area, there is a resident work force of police professionals able and (apparently) eager to provide all the police services the people need.

Has the team police concept worked in practice as well as theory predicted? Preliminary data indicate that it has. Raymond Galvin says of Holyoke's Team Police Unit:

> We can stand behind it as a partially proven, successful, organizational model. I want to see it done here again with greater controls. Unfortunately, there was no ability in this department to evaluate itself. The new grant extending the program to other wards calls for a full-time evaluation staff. Hopefully, all the questions we still have, because of insufficient data, will be answered then.[8]

> However [Angell adds], we do know that things aren't any worse in any area, and in the areas we predicted they would be better they are, in fact, better. In no instance was there a negative attitude change. Whereas in our control ward, Ward Two, which has identical demographic characteristics, attitudes were either the same or worse towards police service. There definitely has been a positive impact by the team police on Ward One.[9]

Michael O'Neill further notes that morale has been very good within the unit. The officers say it is easier to do the job, and for that matter, easier simply to walk down the street. One highly significant indication of improved morale is the statistic relating to sick leave. Within the Team Police—where the caseload per man was double the caseload of the police operating out of central headquarters—sick leave averaged 1.3 days per month per man. In the remainder of the department the average was 4.3 sick leave days per month per man.

To measure changes in community sentiment, evaluations were made in December 1970 and then again during the summer of 1971, after the Team Police Unit had been operative for six months. Significant opinion shifts were found, with differences ranging upward of 10 and 15 percent in some categories.

The portion of respondents in Ward One who agreed with the statement "The police in our ward are better than police in other wards" rose from 18 to 32 percent. In the same period, favorable replies in Ward Two, with police operating in the traditional preventive patrol pattern, declined from 13 to 5 percent. In Ward One the segment agreeing with the statement "The police in our ward do more work than they have to" grew from 26 to 34 percent, whereas the comparable figures in Ward Two decreased from 25 to 13 percent. Given the statement "The police in our ward are anxious to help people," those in Ward One who agreed went from 62 to 67 percent. In Ward Two, there was a decline from 61 to 40 percent.

All these statistics strongly suggest that the attitudes of people toward police service are relative. With the arrival elsewhere in the city of the Team Police and their citizen-oriented attitude and demeanor, the people in the control ward reported a significant lessening of approval for the police service they were receiving. They could observe that a more responsive police service than perhaps had been believed possible was indeed obtainable. Thus, in one significant opinion shift, the portion of people in Ward Two who agreed with the statement "The police in our ward are polite" decreased from 72 to 52 percent.

Despite the impressive data on opinion changes, the

evaluators hesitate to consider the program to be an un-qualified success. Their reluctance stems from the diffi-culty they had overcoming inertia in mounting the program of data collection. A considerable amount of antiteam feeling manifested itself not only within the department (as resistance to data collection and to the retrieval of data that did exist) but also outside the department. For exam-ple, certain city aldermen shared with some higher police administrators the view that "real" police work was being undermined. However, the program had the unqualified and enthusiastic support of the mayor, who believed, despite such resistance, that the program was a success.

There was also an independent appraisal of the pro-gram, conducted by police chiefs from Oakland, Califor-nia; Dayton, Ohio; North St. Paul, Minnesota; Reno, Nevada; and Miamisburg, Ohio. Their evaluation, in the summer of 1971, consisted of interviews with fifteen team members, seven Holyoke officers from the traditional structure, a group selected by duty command officers, and also through personal observation (e.g., riding in cruisers and otherwise participating in the life of the department). The five chiefs concluded that in technical and profes-sional proficiency, personal motivation, ability to interact as human beings, and other like factors, the Team Police officers rated generally higher than other Holyoke police. According to Jack Goss:

> Their impressions were that the attitude of TPU offi-cers towards their job was markedly better than the regular police, that the community attitude towards their police had improved incredibly, to the extent that they were actually *possessive* about the team, and that in basic police skills, the team was re-sponding more effectively than the rest of the department.[10]

This conclusion appears to be borne out by the available data on police performance.

With respect to "Clientele opinions about response time," residents of Ward One who thought that police arrived within six minutes of being called numbered 54 percent, whereas in Ward Two, only 26 percent had the same perception.

"Clientele opinions about the Police Department after the incident" refers to interviews undertaken with people who had actually requested police service. Here the attitude of 63 percent in Ward One was favorable, with 12 percent unfavorable. In Ward Two, the attitude of 49 percent was favorable, with 25 percent unfavorable.

Finally, the evaluators sought to determine people's opinions about the overall police service. The response in Ward One was 62 percent favorable, 6 percent unfavorable. In Ward Two 43 percent were favorable, 26 percent unfavorable. In summation, Galvin says:

> There are a lot of plusses. But in my view [the team police concept] hasn't proven itself completely. I think it ought to be continued as an experiment. There are all sorts of problems here in Holyoke having to do with who likes the program and who doesn't, who's in control and who has lost control, disagreements about how much supervision the men need, and things like that. When you talk about inserting anything into the police field you expect a change shock, so when you're talking about anything as radical as this is, you're not only going to run into that sort of thing, but into opposition from accepted hierarchical concepts in terms of rank and command and title and that sort of thing.
>
> Also, despite all we've learned about this model, we don't yet know if it can be put in someplace where it's really busy. The five chiefs who came in to study the program were all impressed that *none* of the

police in Holyoke were terribly busy. There's just not that much crime. In Oakland, we're taking two beats, and I mean *busy* beats, and we're going to model police teams on this organizational format as far as we can. The question is, to put it bluntly, how much democracy are we going to be able to get away with? One of the big problems of the highly structured classical bureaucracy is that the men in it have already been indoctrinated to that being the proper way to perform.

I think John Angell's model can work presently, but it's going to be very painful. It is very difficult to get the administrators to take a chance with *any* experiment. Also, after the initial blush of success, when everybody wants to be a part of it, then the problem is the tedious, day-after-day operation, when the men in the team have to assume responsibilities that they could get away without assuming before, in the traditional structure, and they slow down. And don't forget, all this time they're not getting encouragement very often from a reticent middle management or brother officers.

But there's no doubt we've made progress. We're just going to have to keep trying and keep trying."

16. Toward a Democratic Police

It is not going to be easy to develop in the United States a police with a democratic manner and bearing and with the philosophy and structure that will sustain the individual officers. Nothing less, however, will suffice. In our view, that goal has been accomplished in Holyoke to a remarkable extent. Yet along with the evaluators of the program, we grant that flaws exist in the operation of Holyoke's Team Police Unit. We feel that the intradepartmental fragmentation over the issue has been unfortunate. We feel

183

that the training received by the members of the unit has been inadequate and that there is insufficient in-service training. Like the evaluators, we feel that the formal advisory groups have been coopted by the police (and Captain Burns, incidentally, agrees). In the light of the progress that has been made, however, we can now believe that this structure, or one like it, can make serious inroads into what otherwise might be seen as an insoluble problem.

We are particularly pleased that resistance to the program has been relatively mild. This we trace to the strong and determined leadership of Mayor Taupier, who describes himself as a conservative but whose sense of the magnitude of the crisis in urban affairs is as keen as any radical's.

Finally, we must note that creating a democratic team police does not by any means require dismissal of all existing personnel. In Holyoke, for example, the seed stock for a democratic team police was present in the same personnel who, only one year earlier, had cruised Ward One as distant, alienated authoritarians. One of them was Patrolman Donaghue, who still carries a bullet in his stomach.

> Why did I volunteer for the TPU? Professionally, I thought it was a good idea, and personally, I thought about it a long time. I probably didn't admit it to myself, but I wanted to show I wasn't afraid to go down to the Flats. Maybe I'm still a little bit jumpy. But it's really a whole different ball game, down here, since the TPU. This is no public relations job. We're for real. And I love it. This is what I always imagined police work was all about.[1]

Although the team policing concept was very effective in a small community like Holyoke, certain problems arose in larger cities like Dayton. The early Dayton Plan was somewhat marred by the inability of the personnel to respond favorably to a bigger, more diversified community. In Dayton the team worked a fairly large area containing some 60,000 inhabitants of widely varied socioeconomic levels, as opposed to the essentially class-homogeneous people in Holyoke's Ward One. Although their studies implied that the new concept worked well in Holyoke, both Angell and Galvin had reservations about its appropriateness in a larger, more crime-ridden locale. Dayton's team program had to be revised by breaking down the area covered into more homogeneous social groupings.

In fact, when members of the Dayton police team unit visited New York's first experimental precinct, they were amazed at the level of the work load. After spending several days riding in the 77th Precinct's radio cars in Brooklyn's high-crime Bedford-Stuyvesant district, they voiced some doubts that their team could operate under such a heavy demand for police services. However, three experimental areas in New York City indicated positive and promising results.

New York's first effort in team policing started January 1, 1971. A section of one of New York's 78 police precincts was designated for this purpose. Led by Sergeant William Ambrose, a team of volunteers operated in the 77th Precinct, under a carefully prescribed mandate from the top command of the department. They were to provide for everyone in the community police service that would reduce crime, fear, and tension. From recent conversations with Sergeant Ambrose it is evident that things are going well. At a recent team meeting we attended, he and his men showed extremely high spirit and enthusiasm. All the members of the group are volunteers, and the waiting list for team membership is a long one. Some of the positive results of the project include a higher rate of arrests for crimes, a reduced need for supervisory and disciplinary procedures, and a healthy desire on the part of the men to fulfill their role with distinction.

Emphasis is on service, community input and interaction, and the development of youth-oriented programs. In addition, increased police presence and reduction in response time, as well as police attention to local needs, have resulted in greater cooperation from the community and diminishing fear of victimization in the streets. Young people have come to know the policemen by name from meetings and casual conversations that inevitably increase confidence and trust in the police. A regular weekly outing for local youth supervised by team members has been especially helpful in developing good police–community relations.

Many precincts in New York have neighborhood police teams operating within a portion of their jurisdictions; but the 34th Precinct, in upper Manhattan, was the first in the city to be organized entirely on the team concept. It is probably the first that did not use volunteers only as participants. In a racially and ethnically integrated area containing about 170,000 people, five police teams were organized to provide what New York State Senator Joseph Zaretzski described as a "pioneering experiment in police decentralization for the purpose of providing better police protection and service. . . ." Senator Zaretzki indicated that ". . . the success of the plan depended on improved citizen cooperation with the police on the neighborhood level, and vice versa."[2]

Although the New York Police Department's team policing experiments are organized on the classical police model (uniforms, ranks, chain of command) and on the legalistic concept of enforcing the law through formal criminal procedures, two other approaches are added. One is the human relations model for improving cooperation by personal involvement; the other is the behavioral approach, which emphasizes motivation and the development of a favorable self-image for the police.

Captain Howard Anderson, the commanding officer of the 34th Precinct, developed some of the management concepts while assigned to the department's Planning Bureau. He found that the program has been well received by the community and that it has shown some exemplary results. Recent figures, he told us, indicate a significant reduction in the number of robbery complaints and a substantial increase in the total number of arrests effected in the precincts. He has also noted a reduction in the time spent in the handling of calls for service (dispatcher assignment to final disposition) from 40 to 23 minutes. This he attributed to improved morale, interest, and self-discipline.[3] Better supervision, more participation in decision-making, and increased teamwork have improved the patrolman's self-esteem and enhanced his image in the community, thereby reducing the likelihood of corruption. His conclusion that the team concept can be adopted for entire precincts on a citywide basis was predicated on general acceptance of the concept by the patrolmen, the public, and the supervisory personnel. All seem to benefit under this plan—the public receives better police service and protection, and the department has the advantage of modern administrative and management methodology.

Tied in with improved relationships often fostered by team policing is another idea that originated in Captain Anderson's command. A resident patrolman has been assigned to the area; he, it is hoped, will provide improved liaison between the police administration and the community.

Afterword

The facts of the police officer's life show that police work almost always involves human interaction, but law-enforcement work comprises only a small part of the work load. A study of citizen calls to the Syracuse, New York, police department for a two-week period in the summer of 1966 revealed that 22 percent of the calls were information gathering, 37.5 percent were service calls, 30.1 percent had to do with order maintenance, and only 10.3 percent concerned law enforcement.[1] These data are confirmed by other studies, and the proportions cited are common knowledge among police administrators, although they rarely acknowledge this. Not until the reality of the police experience becomes the basis for the way we identify the police officer, however, can we achieve the reorientation that will produce the police professional who functions and is perceived as part of the network of social service assistance agencies.

When the police are no longer seen primarily as punitive agents, and when the police cease to think of themselves primarily as agents for a punitive system, they will not behave punitively except when this becomes necessary to make an arrest. The rest of the time, the policeman will function as a manager of neighborhood conflicts.

We imagine an officer who is a skilled professional, respected as such in the precinct in which he works. He will be dealing with matters involving law enforcement about 10 to 15 percent of the time, as he is now; and of course he will have received at least equivalent training in handling these matters. But crime fighting as such does not absorb the major part of his time or his energy, nor does the crime-fighter image constitute the mainstay of his identity.

To accomplish the change envisioned, we must first implement ways of changing the patrolman's view of himself. We can start by instituting hierarchic, bureaucratic reforms that will enhance the patrolman's self-image; that is, we can change the way his superiors see him and treat him. We can also redefine his aims and functions by reorganizing police priorities to emphasize conflict management within the patrolman's area of responsibility. Third, we can train him properly. And in addition to better training, a well-thought-out recruitment philosophy is critical to bringing about the officer's psychological maturity and preparing him to see himself in an objective, professional role.

Let us begin with the question of recruitment. Today, from the moment we suggest to a young man that he might want to be a policeman, we emphasize that he will be a member of a semimilitaristic, armed, authoritarian force. Police are commonly identified as having in their psychological makeup large components of suspicion, prejudice, cynicism, moralism, aggression, conventionality, and other personality factors that typify the authoritarian character. Yet it is also true that policemen rank high in the desire for security and social service. Consequently, the same basic manpower pool from which personnel are drawn for the various social service agencies could just as easily provide recruits for police agencies.

Traditionally, the training that follows recruitment has pursued the theme of the policeman as an enforcer of the law. Furthermore, it tends to be nonparticipatory training —a system of lectures transmitting a body of information which, the student learns on joining the force, is not to be taken seriously. Every rookie is told shortly after being sworn in that "you can't go by the book." The training and education of a young police officer must bear some relationship to what he experiences on the street. He must be taught not as a mere recipient of information, but as a participant who needs to develop specific skills, particularly the capacity to successfully negotiate a diversity of human encounters.

To develop these basic police skills, the trainee should be repeatedly required to simulate the street experience. In the process, he should be encouraged to develop his own concept of how his approach to police duties produces reactions ranging from approval and compliance to anger, hostility, and assault. Prominent among the training tools that will encourage the development of these skills are programs mentioned earlier, such as human interaction training, and specific skill development programs, such as family crisis intervention training or simulation games that reproduce the street situation accurately.

At present the police officer is not properly trained for a work load that necessitates a high degree of autonomy and discretion, as well as repeated contact with the public. Nor is he encouraged to function in that manner when he receives his first assignment. Throughout most of his career, in fact, the police officer lives in a world of power, yet one in which he himself has no power. The patrolman has not helped to formulate the policies he is required to enforce, and he is given little latitude in interpreting them.

The education, training, and in-service development of a police professional who can cope with the complexity of the urban streets must increasingly emphasize emotional maturity, good judgment, a personal sense of responsibility, and tolerance for diversity. These are traits that tend to accompany increased self-knowledge and a rise in the level of education. We are moving in that direction anyway. More and more we will be recruiting at a higher level of education and expecting officers to continue their educational efforts. Early in 1972 in New York a 10-year program was proposed by Commissioner Murphy, which envisioned that by June 1972 all police candidates would be required to have completed 16 college credits. By June 1974 the requirement would be raised to 32 credits, or one full year of college. Similarly, for promotion to superior officer ranks, two-year college requirements were to be instituted by June 1975 (for captain), by June 1976 (for lieutenant), and by June 1977 (for sergeant). Three years later, in each of these categories, a baccalaureate degree would be required for promotion. The ultimate fate of this program is now in doubt because of opposition to it by the police line organizations.

Given a well-educated police professional who has the attitudes previously described, we must put this individual in a department that will accord him the status he deserves. We need to consider such intangible elements as the responsibility and autonomy the officer is given, the respect he receives, the salary he is paid, and the amount of attention his needs are given.

The first step toward attaining such a goal is the creation inside the police structure of an office that functions in all matters of policy, internal discipline, and the like as an ombudsman for patrolmen. (There should be a parallel office functioning on behalf of ranking officers.) The new office would first of all represent the officers in grievance matters. One of the policeman's prime and in our view most justified complaints is that no machinery now exists to deal with well-intentioned errors. There is no provision, either in the law or in the rules and regulations of the police organization, for a police officer to make an honest mistake and later acknowledge it. Consequently, if he errs in dealing with people, he is almost certain to resort to some legitimizing tactic to justify himself. Sometimes in the heat of a situation, when tempers are flaring, the police response may be influenced by an officer's concern for his safety, by his inexperience, or by poor judgment, and we must be able to distinguish inappropriate but excusable behavior from police actions that are ill-intentioned or illegal.

The police officer feels (and is) unprotected, and that partly explains why veteran officers immediately advise all new arrivals of the code of secrecy. In the absence of effective grievance machinery, it is clearly to the advantage of the entire force for everybody to keep his mouth shut no matter what happens. Therefore, not only is the institution of effective internal grievance machinery likely to relax this fearful conspiracy somewhat, but it will also tend to restore public confidence in the state of police ethics. Now more than ever, major efforts must be made to reassure people that police administrators are not cynically content to let police corruption pass as a necessary evil.

Lateral entry of civilians into the criminal justice system at every level is desirable, especially in an office functioning for the benefit of the police officer.

Let us now return to the subject of police mistakes. There is no provision for correcting mistakes because, historically, police have functioned as an arm of the state, and the state, as the embodiment of the laws, made no mistakes. There is little disagreement about the expectation that the policeman will protect property on behalf of the state or apprehend order-disturbers on behalf of public order. Most police–community problems that have to do with grievances for abuse of authority, unnecessary use of force, or false arrest, stem from the discrepancy between the community's perception of the police and the perception of the police itself. Police who continue to see themselves solely as law enforcers will remain at a distance from communities that are evolving a concept of the police that is grounded in the idea of community service. We do not see how effective grievance machinery, fair to the public and fair to the police, could exist without dealing with this fundamental problem. The policeman, even though he represents the state, must be allowed to make mistakes; thus the police, as an instrument of the state, must admit that mistakes can be made, and there must be provision for the patrolman to learn from his mistakes. The most useful framework for acknowledging this admission is citizen participation in grievance machinery on the one hand, and protection for officers who make honest mistakes on the other.

Often police officers must make split-second decisions; occasionally human life is at stake, and under certain conditions police officers are empowered to kill. The policeman's responsibilities are grave and even with the best intentions, errors are made. A consensus has been developing against the use of lethal force except for crimes where actual or threatened deadly force has occurred. This is a relatively new trend, as even a cursory look at the history of policing will show. Nevertheless, force continues to be a weapon in the police arsenal, and communities will vary in their desire to see it used. This being the case, the grievance machinery that protects the policeman from unjustified complaints and honest errors must have the support of the community, and it must enjoy unlimited credibility. It must also reflect the community's wishes with respect to the use of force. Thus we return to our suggestion that the ombudsman's office ought to be composed of civilians and police.

If such a police ombudsman's office exists, it should operate jointly with a community ombudsman's office (again, staffed jointly with civilians and service officers). Thus we would have a police–community grievance structure competent to ensure that each element in the triangle (police, community, police administration) feels protected and has trust in the integrity of the adjudications of the various ombudsmen's offices. The total system, which would be a police–community grievance board—should not restrict itself to complaints against individual police officers or against police administrators; it should consider any element of the criminal justice system or city service that needs looking into. There is no particular reason for singling out police, and there are many reasons for integrating grievances.

We envison the structure of the grievance system retaining centralized (staff) functions, perhaps under a citywide ombudsman, but running in a decentralized mode with respect to specific complaints. The precinct grievance office would have primary operational responsibility.

We would be less than candid if we did not confess that the ombudsman concept raises a number of difficult questions—ones that might best be answered through a joint police–community committee appointed and assigned to explore and recommend soiutions and answers.

For example, who will do the investigating? who decides? (majority rule on the panel? does the police commissioner have a veto?), and what happens if it is determined that a policeman erred in the performance of his duties? In addition, where does one draw the line between what an ombudsman can handle, what should be allowed to remain within the police department, what should go to the courts, and who makes these decisions?

These questions are not easily answered but we must start somewhere.

A man who works almost autonomously within a system so responsive to community needs, and at the level of professionalism described, deserves considerably higher pay than policemen get today. The reward structure for the police professional will have to be altered as well, so that benefits for specific performance (e.g., making arrests) do not overbalance rewards for the overall manner in which the community is policed. Thus the incidence of complaint-provoking behavior will tend to decrease, and the matter of police–community relations will become intrinsic to every contact the police has with the people.

Finally, it seems highly likely to the authors that a police thus empowered will be less isolated and secretive, less cynical, less dependent on peers for emotional support, and more responsive to the idea of civilian participation throughout the criminal justice system—it will, in short, be able to perform skillfully and with high self-esteem a dynamic, evolving police mission.

On an individual basis, we will settle for nothing less than a police officer who is respected in the community in which he works. In the fine old tradition of the romantic police imagination, we are talking about a cop who is proud of his badge and what it stands for: his willingness to help the weak and the innocent when others might turn their heads, and to assert his strength on behalf of community peace and order.

He is not a brusque, ill-tempered man of little skill who is constantly on hand to interfere with your pleasures, as long as nobody is hurt by them; yet is not around when you are being mugged. By no means. He is the community's conflict manager. The area's residents know very well that he can be depended on to come around and settle disputes that arise in the community, generally to everybody's satisfaction.

Mr. and Mrs. Whatstheirname are throwing things at each other again? Call the cop. There's nobody else who can get those two calmed down as quickly.

Noisy altercation between the grocer and a gang of young Latins? Call a cop. He plays basketball with those kids two nights a week. They'll trust him to be even-handed and not take sides in the dispute, except to resolve it peacefully.

But what's he doing playing basketball on duty? What

about the criminals? Why isn't he out catching criminals?

Well, on a number of levels, playing basketball with the neighborhood kids can have precisely that result. With all due respect to the literary image of the man in blue on the street corner, sternly eyeing miscreants, that is not at all the most meaningful way in which "criminals" are "caught." Managing conflicts in a community involves many more subtle and more difficult tasks.

Imagine a police officer whose informants are so numerous and so well-respected in the community that a heroin pusher cannot last a day in his precinct without being identified. Imagine a precinct in which the community is confident that it has a voice at precinct headquarters:

> Officer, we need your help getting a street light put in at the corner where the kid got hit by a car last week.

> Officer, I can't figure out why my welfare check never showed up. I need you to call them for me.

> Officer, this is the third day now I can't get any heat and my kids are freezing. Arrest my landlord.

> Officer, we're going to be demonstrating in front of the Defense Department. We'd like you to come down and monitor it.

Doesn't sound like real police work, you say? On the contrary. Nothing works better to reduce conflicts in a precinct than constant and deep involvement in the community's problems that are due to lack of services, whether from government or from private parties. Naturally, then, most of the department's effort in terms of time, energy, manpower, skill development, and training should be directed at this area.

As a result, this officer has been trained in special

human interaction skills that enable him to reduce the tensions whenever he appears on the scene. He knows what people are like, and he knows how to find out what's bugging them. He will sit down and talk to them for an hour to calm them, if necessary; or if the situation requires making a call or two, he knows the numbers.

He's good at his job partly because he knows his area so well. He has, after all, liaison responsibility with the community. There is frequent contact. The officer realizes that knowing what is on the minds and in the hearts of the people is the best peace maintenance weapon he has. He touches bases all the time. He knows what dissident elements are thinking, and they know that he'll stay neutral even though he does not accept their principles. They in turn respect him for doing his job although they disagree with him frequently.

In fact, however, militant groups often find that they have some ideas in common with the police, and they are working on them together. For example, police are keeping drug dealers away from black children. They're in court pressing a joint claim for damages against a landlord who never can be reached when the heat goes out in the dead of winter. They're making a joint survey of the precinct regarding racial prejudice with respect to employment practices.

In other words, our conflict manager bears a great commitment to the community and its needs, and his rapport with the people who live there is considerable.

This is no fly-by-night tough with a nightstick who comes in from out of town to lay down the law. He is not apart from the community. He is a part of it. Largely for that reason, he has been able to do his job with the help of resources within the community that simply were not available to the old-style cop. People sometimes come to him and identify problems that are not due to erupt for weeks or months. But he's getting so much input from the community that many of the problems are solved long before they become a source of disorder.

As often as not, important information about building tensions comes directly to the station house. This is not too surprising, considering how much time the people of the neighborhood pass there. The station house is right on the street; it's accessible, it's open, and all sorts of community activities take place in the building. The youngsters find the cops fun to kid around with. And they level with them.

This officer is a man who has respect because he's earned it, not because he demands it.

He doesn't need to tell people of his value to the community. They know it.

He doesn't have to prove that he has authority. The people give it to him because there is nothing he likes better than to help them iron out their problems, and he is a skilled professional at that trade.

He is not there to enforce laws against the people of the community. He is there to keep their peace, to keep them secure from harm in person and in property. That is why they give him the job and the authority.

Notes and References

CHAPTER 1

1. *Police Training and Performance Study: Project Report Submitted to the New York City Police Department and the Law Enforcement Assistance Administration* (December 1969), p. 77. Indicates that the average IQ of recruits during a seven-year period (1962–1969) varied from 111.71 to 93.19. This range falls within the parameters of average intelligence.

2. N. A. Watson and J. W. Sterling, *Police and Their Opinions* (Washington, D.C., International Association of Chiefs of Police, 1969), p. 116.

3. William A. Westley, *Violence and the Police* (Cambridge, Mass., The M.I.T. Press, 1970), p. 205; John H. McNamara, "Uncertainties in Police Work; Recruits' Background and Training," *The Police: Six Sociological Essays*, David J. Bordua, ed. (New York, John Wiley and Sons, 1967), pp. 193–194.

4. Joseph D. Lohman and Gordon E. Misner, *The Police and the Community, Field Surveys IV* (Washington, D.C., U.S. Government Printing Office, 1966), p. 193; James Q. Wilson, *Varieties of Police Behavior* (Cambridge, Mass., Harvard University Press, 1968), pp. 33–34; and Watson and Sterling, *op. cit.*, p. 106.

5. Arthur Niederhoffer, *Behind the Shield* (Garden City, N.Y., Doubleday, 1967), p. 3.

6. Martin Symonds, "Emotional Hazards of Police Work," *American Journal of Psychoanalysis*, Vol. XXX, No. 2, 1970, p. 156.

7. *Police Training and Performance Study, op. cit.*, p. 448.

8. *New York City Police Department Police Academy Recruit Training Syllabus* (July 1971), p. ii.

9. Peter Cowen, "Graft Held Fact of Life in Boston," *Boston Globe*, October 2, 1972.

10. *Police: Report of the National Advisory Commission on Criminal Justice Standards and Goals* (January 1973), p. 396.

11. *Ibid.*

12. *Ibid.*

CHAPTER 2

1. James Vorenberg, "Nixon and Crime—Four Years Later," *Boston Globe*, October 1, 1972.

2. Jerome H. Skolnick, *Justice Without Trial: Law Enforcement in a Democratic Society* (New York, John Wiley and Sons, 1967), p. 45 ff.

CHAPTER 3

1. Conversation with authors.

2. *Ibid.*

3. Philip Taft and Philip Ross, "American Labor Violence: Its
    Causes, Character, and Outcome," in Hugh Davis Graham
    and Ted Robert Gurr, eds., *The History of Violence in
    America: Historical and Comparative Perspectives, A Re-
    port Submitted to the National Commission on Causes and
    Prevention of Violence* (New York, Praeger, 1969), p. 359.
    Also available in Bantam paperback.

4. *Report of the National Advisory Commission on Civil Dis-
    orders* (New York, Bantam, 1968), p. 299.

5. James Baldwin, *Nobody Knows My Name* (New York, Dell,
    1962), pp 65–67.

6. James Q. Wilson, *Varieties of Police Behavior* (Cambridge,
    Mass., Harvard University Press, 1968), p. 188.

7. John Bainbridge, "Constable," *New Yorker*, August 14,
    1971.

CHAPTER 4

1. Richard Maxwell Brown, "Historical Patterns of Violence in
    America," in Graham and Gurr, *op. cit.*, p. 67.

2. *Ibid.*, p. 68.

CHAPTER 5

1. "The Police and the Community," *Task Force Report: The
    Police* (Washington, D.C., U.S. Government Printing Office,
    1967), Chapter six.

2. *Ibid.*, p. 123.

3. Conversation with authors.

4. Herbert Jenkins, *Keeping the Peace* (New York, Harper &
    Row, 1970), pp. 97–98.

CHAPTER 6

1. Terry Ann Knopf, *Youth Patrol: An Experiment in Commu-
    nity Participation* (Waltham, Mass., Brandeis University,
    The Lemburg Center for the Study of Violence, 1969), p. 7.

2. *Ibid.*, p. 23.

3. *Ibid.*, p. 36.

CHAPTER 7

1. Speech by Patrick Murphy delivered for the New York Police Academy, October 6, 1971.
2. *Ibid.*
3. *Annual Report,* City of New York Police Department, Office of the Deputy Commissioner—Community Relations, 1968.
4. "Police Ride-Along is Liked by Chief," *World Herald* (Omaha, Nebraska), January 13, 1971.
5. "Police Community Relations," *Star* (Omaha, Nebraska), September 24, 1971.
6. Robert D. McFadden, "Civilian Observers Ride Prowl Cars in City Test," *New York Times*, July 27, 1971.
7. *World Herald, supra.*
8. Lee P. Brown, "Typology-Orientation of Police–Community Relations Programs," *The Police Chief*, Vol. XXXVIII, No. 3 (March 1971), p. 20.

CHAPTER 8

1. Michael Harrington, *The Other America, Poverty in the United States* (Baltimore, Penguin Books, 1963), p. 23.
2. Col. Robert M. Igleburger, *Proposal for Team Policing Project* (Dayton, Ohio, unpublished), p. 2.
3. *Ibid.*, p. 1.
4. Conversation with authors.

CHAPTER 9

1. Lee P. Brown, "Typology-Orientation of Police–Community Relations Programs," *The Police Chief*, Vol. XXXVIII, No. 3 (March 1971), p. 20.
2. Conversation with authors.
3. *Annual Report*, City of New York Police Department, Office of the Deputy Commissioner—Community Relations, 1968, p. 12.
4. Edward J. Rosenbluh and William A. Reichart, "Small Group Interaction Approach to Police Community Relations," unpublished, p. 7.

5. "Preliminary Proposal for Training Personnel, Jackson-ville Police Department," *Anti-Defamation League Memo*, March 1969.

6. "Police–Community Relations Program," *Anti-Defamation League, Memo*, April 15, 1971.

7. Rosenbluh and Reichart, *supra.*, p. 7.

8. "Evaluation of Police–Youth Encounter Group Workshops in the City of Rochester," *Behavioral Science Consulting Associates* (September 1, 1970), p. 129.

9. Gordon W. Allport, *The Nature of Prejudice* (New York, Doubleday-Anchor, 1958), p. 382.

10. *Ibid.*, p. 283–284.

CHAPTER 10

1. James Q. Wilson, *Varieties of Police Behavior* (Cam-bridge, Mass., Harvard University Press, 1968), p. 24.

2. Morton Bard and Bernard Berkowitz, "Family Disturbance as a Police Function," in *Law Enforcement Science and Technology*, Vol. II, S. I. Cohn, ed. (I.I.T. Research Insti-tute, Washington, Thompson Book Co., 1968), p. 566.

3. Wilson, *supra.*

4. City of New York Police Department, Crime Analysis Bureau, 1972.

5. Ronald Sullivan, "Violence, Like Charity, Begins at Home," *New York Times Magazine*, November 24, 1968.

6. Morton Bard and Bernard Berkowitz, "Training Police as Specialists in Family Crisis Intervention," for the National Institute of Law Enforcement and Criminal Justice (Wash-ington, D.C., U.S. Government Printing Office, 1970), p. iii.

7. *Ibid.*, p. 6.

8. *Ibid.*

9. *Ibid.*, p. 17.

10. *Ibid.*, p. 18.

11. Sullivan, *supra.*

12. Bernard Berkowitz, "Alternatives to Violence," paper pre-sented to the American Orthopsychiatric Association (New York, March 30–April 2, 1969), p. 5.

13. *Guidelines For Demonstrations* (Police Department, City of New York), p. 8.

14. Berkowitz, *supra.*, p. 3.

15. *Ibid.*

16. Morton Bard and Bernard Berkowitz, "A Community Psychology Consultation Program in Police Family Crisis Intervention: Preliminary Impressions," *The International Journal of Social Psychiatry*, Vol. XV, No. 1 (Winter 1968–1969), p. 215.

CHAPTER 12

1. Alex Poinsett, "Dilemma of Black Policemen," *Ebony,* May 1971. Other quotes in chapter from same source.

CHAPTER 13

1. William A. Westley, *Violence and the Police* (Cambridge, Mass., The M.I.T. Press, 1970), p. 122.

2. Albert J. Reiss, Jr., *The Police and the Public* (New Haven, Conn., Yale University Press, 1971), p. 149.

3. *Ibid.*, p. 147.

4. Albert J. Reiss, Jr., "Police Brutality—Answers to Key Questions," *Trans-Action*, Vol. 5, No. 8, (July/August, 1968), p. 11.

5. Westley, *op. cit.*, p. 107.

6. *Police Training and Performance Study: Project Report Submitted to the New York City Police Department and the Law Enforcement Assistance Administration* (December 1969), p. 50.

7. Westley, *op. cit.*, p. 179.

8. *Ibid.*, p. 49.

9. Bernard Cohen and Jan M. Chaiken, "Police Background Characteristics and Performance: Summary" (The New York City Rand Institute, May 1972), p. 13.

CHAPTER 14

1. William A. Westley, "The Image of Police," *New York Times*, November 15, 1971.

2. Patrick V. Murphy and Peter B. Bloch, "Beat Commander,"

Search, A Report from the Urban Institute, Vol. 1, No. 1 (January–February, 1971), p. 3.

3. Robert M. Parich, "Murphy Urges People-to-People Police," *The Detroit News*, December 15, 1971.

4. *Ibid.*

5. "Operation Neighborhood" (Office of Public Information, City of New York Police Department).

6. *Ibid.*

7. "Basic Car Plan" (Office of the Chief of Police, Community Relations Section, Los Angeles Police Department, February 1971), p. 1.

8. John Griffin, *Report* (Holyoke, Mass., Holyoke Police Department, unpublished).

9. "Police Relations Plan a Success, Chief Says," *Los Angeles Times,* October 7, 1970.

10. "Basic Car Plan," *supra.*, p. 7.

11. Col. Robert M. Igleburger, *Proposal for Team Policing Project* (Dayton, Ohio, unpublished), Appendix A: The Generalist/Specialist as a Police Officer.

12. *Ibid.*, p. 3.

13. *Ibid.*, p. 7.

14. *Ibid.*, p. 8.

15. Conversation with authors.

CHAPTER 15

1–11. All notes from conversations with authors.

CHAPTER 16

1. Conversation with authors.

2. Joseph Zaretzki, Minority Leader, New York State Senate, *Report to My Constituents: Police Protection*, March 1971.

3. Conversation with authors.

AFTERWORD

1. O. Wilson, *Varieties of Police Behavior* (Cambridge, Mass., Harvard University Press, 1968), p. 18.

Index